The Word of the Cross
in a World of Glory

Other books in the Lutheran Voices series

LUTHERAN
VOICES

The Word
of the Cross
in a World
of Glory

Philip Ruge-Jones

Augsburg Fortress

Minneapolis

THE WORD OF THE CROSS IN A WORLD OF GLORY

Library of Congress Cataloging-in-Publication Data
Ruge-Jones, Philip, 1962-
The Word of the cross in a world of glory / Philip Ruge-Jones.
    p. cm. — (Lutheran voices series)
ISBN 978-0-8066-8005-7 (alk. paper)
1. Jesus Christ—Crucifixion. 2. Christianity—Influence. 3. Christianity and culture. I. Title.
BT453.R86 2008
261.09—dc22   2007036810

12   11   10   09   08   1   2   3   4   5   6   7   8   9   10

To my parents, Lola and Marty Ruge
Thanks for loving me where I'm at—

Contents

Acknowledgments

I have become profoundly aware while writing this book of the countless people who have shaped me in this life. Many are named in this book; many more are not. I trust that you know who you are and how grateful I am to you.

Special thanks to Texas Lutheran University for the tremendous support I have received in that community of faith and learning. Your gift of a sabbatical made it possible for me to write down the thoughts that you read here.

Thank you to the storytellers and scholars who take part with me in the NOBS Seminar each summer. Together we have asked how the spoken and performed words that we have in the Bible shaped early communities of faith. Traces of that conversation can be found in the first chapter and at www.nobsseminar.org.

I am grateful to my editor at Augsburg Fortress, who made this, my first book, a much better book. Thanks, Susan, for guiding me with much wisdom and grace!

On a very personal note, thanks to my wife, Lori, and our children, Lucas and Luisa, for supporting me during the writing of this book and the living of this life. When all else is falling apart, I can always count on you.

Thanks, too, to my parents, Lola and Marty Ruge, whose story you will read in the third chapter. You were the first to speak to me the word of the cross, and this book is dedicated to you.

Finally, I am grateful to you readers, for what is the worth of a story if there is no one to hear it? You've heard my stories, now I welcome the opportunity to hear yours. Please feel free to contact me at pruge-jones@tlu.edu.

Introduction

Ho, everyone who thirsts, come to the waters;
And you that have no money, come, buy and eat!
Come buy wine and milk without money and without price.
Why do you spend your money on that which is not bread,
and your labor for that which does not satisfy?

Isaiah 55:1-2

Christians claim, and have claimed since the first century, that the glory of God is revealed in the self-giving life and brutal death of God's only son, Jesus, the Christ. This glory that is strange in deed is, indeed, strange–incomprehensible, in fact—to a world that glories in power, prestige, profits, and certitude.

To see glory in the naked Christ hanging powerlessly upon a cross is folly to the world. But Christians are drawn to that cross, holding fast to the claim that God is up to something truly glorious in the life and death of this one who lived out the power of love instead of selling out to the love of power. Paul, the apostle, proclaimed the message of this reconciling and transforming power—the word of the cross—to any and all who would hear. Others, too, proclaimed this good news—this gospel—bringing their hearers close to the crucified Jesus where the word of the cross challenged some, comforted others, but left no life untouched.

The word of the cross declares brokenness in the very heart of God who doesn't remain distant from us but enters into the shattered realities of our lives in order to make all things new. God's glory is not a distant shining in the heavens but is present in the midst of profound darkness here on earth. In the real struggles of our lives—in betrayal, abuse, and death—God acts to bring about new life. Betrayal gives way to renewed relationships, abuse to love, death to life. God enters into our suffering and the suffering of our world today so that we will be less likely to inflict suffering upon others tomorrow. This powerful declaration comes to us today as *word*—word of the cross. But this word is neither passive nor complicit in the world's suffering. This word of the cross carries within it the power of God's reconciling and transforming love, available to us and also challenging us. We will explore this challenge in the chapters of this book. But first a reminder of what must be our understandings of terms like *power, weakness, brokenness,* and *glory.*

My closest colleague at Texas Lutheran University, Dr. Carolyn Schneider, insists that this is what makes the Bible trustworthy for her. It is a "word of the cross" that comes to us not as a fanciful tale of whole, intact, glorified life but rather as a witness to the suffering and brokenness that defines our humanity and our world. Hearing Jesus cry out from the cross in terror and frustration, "My God, my God, why have you forsaken me?" makes this story credible for her. She can relate it to her life and the brokenness that is a continual guest in the only world we know. Although God enters our broken world through fragile flesh, the flesh of Jesus, God continues to shape the world—and us—through fragile word, the word of the cross. This is not the false word of the cross, carried forth by conquerors and backed by the sword. It is a word that is as vulnerable and open to attack as Jesus was on the cross. Yet, this word pulls us in, shakes us up, and wins the world over by its very weakness.

How can weakness defeat power as the world understands it? God's power is not the power of empires and military might. Neither is it measured in profits or prestige. We misguided humans too often equate power with control of our own destiny and that of others. We seek identity in glorious illusions, relying on products that promise to numb our pain and distract us from the brokenness in our lives. We even try to claim achievements to justify our existence before God, hoping for certainty in places where God does not offer it. We divide our complex world into "good guys" and "bad guys" so we can blame the "bad guys" and absolve ourselves from responsibility.

But none of this is glory as Jesus has defined it for us. Jesus' glory is powerful in his weakness. Jesus comforts us, not with certainty, but with a vision of opportunities and hope. Jesus calls us to step outside of our own self-centered and safe view of how things are, to stand with him on the edges and join hands with all of God's children. Jesus celebrates not our achievements but the good news of God's extravagant love. Jesus promises to make all things new.

Time and again God has raised up witnesses to speak of the power of God in Christ Jesus to a world hungry for food that satisfies. Some hold a place in history; others only in our hearts. In this book you will meet several witnesses who shared this peculiar reconciling and transforming word of the cross with me and you will be invited to identify those who spoke—and continue to speak—God's word to you in your life.

What might the church do to help Christians encounter the challenge of the word of the cross? How might the suffering we embrace lessen the suffering we participate in inflicting on others? My hope is that as we journey together through the coming chapters, we will accept the challenges the word of the cross puts before us, and in so doing discover the true richness of God's glory in Jesus.

Faith comes from what is heard.
Romans 10:17

1

The Word of the Cross in the New Testament

In the opening chapters of Genesis, God speaks. And when God speaks, things happen. The skies open. Plants bloom. Animals take their first stumbling steps. Man and woman reflect God's image. All is good because God says so. From beginning to end, the Bible witnesses to the God who enters into our lives through speech as well as through action. God acts most dramatically in Jesus, sending the "Word made flesh" to live with us (John 1:14).

Most believers in the early communities of faith did not encounter the Word of God captured in ink on paper as we do today. Rather, they heard God's Word spoken with a multitude of inflections traveling from the mouth of one believer to the ears of another, or to a whole community of believers at one time. The Word made flesh was delivered by flesh and blood.

The Word was not for them a source of information but the source of their spiritual formation. Through the spoken Word, God created and recreated a people after God's own heart. By the most generous estimates, even in the best of ancient times maybe ten percent of people could read; the Word of God was heard, not read. It wasn't one's eyes but one's ears that served as the doorway to faith. "Faith comes from what is heard," the Apostle Paul declared (Rom. 10:17).

It's easy to forget this when Bibles are everywhere. We carry our leather bound copy of Scripture with us to church where more copies are available next to the hymnals in the pew racks. We forget that it wasn't always this way. For early believers the Word of God wasn't bound in leather. It was unbounded, free. The Word proclaimed rang in people's ears, resounding from hill and household. This Word changed things. The Word changes things still.

I type these words to you in the long shadow of tall bookcases filled with books I've read and books I've yet to read. I am a teacher and I live my life reading words, but printed words have left their mark on you, too. Yet before we could read, other words created us. Our mothers sang us lullabies. Siblings called us by name. Our own first murmurings shaped grandma's lips into a smile. Even after our eyes learned to decipher stories of green eggs and ham, our ears still felt the power of the spoken word, sometimes with great shame ("fatty, fatty, two by four") and sometimes with great joy ("I like you. Will you play with me?").

Today we read God's Word, often silently. But we need to remember that it wasn't always this way. For millennia God's Word was flung aloud with gusto. People not only heard, they actually felt the impact of God's Word.

What do I mean?

In the evenings, my son and I often enjoy some snuggle time after he's tucked in for the night. We both look forward to this precious father and son time at the end of the day. One night when he was about five years old, Lucas took much longer than usual getting ready for bed, so it was late when he finally got settled in and I had things I needed to do. As I kissed him good night, Lucas asked, "Dad, are you gonna snuggle?" "No!" I said, "It took so long to get you into bed that there's no time left for snuggling. I have a stack of papers waiting to be graded! Maybe tomorrow night." A brief pause, and then, "OK, Dad. I was just thinking . . . we haven't had much father and son time lately."

I felt the impact of those words as if I had been slapped. They were words flung not to inform me, but to form me; to shape me in my relationship with my son. As you can guess, the stack of papers waited.

The words of the Bible are like that: they are spoken with the intent of shaping us. The commands, poems, stories, and images of Scripture give rise to new ways of seeing and being in the Word. The words give rise to transformed lives.

Imagine holding the Bible to your ear. Listen closely and you will hear particular words spoken to particular communities. Imagine these words that are so important for your life and mine heard in the contexts in which they were first spoken. Sound, unlike print, is fragile, even weak; it is here one minute and gone the next. It is not a bronze vessel but an earthen one. Yet sound impacts its hearers.

Some of the earliest words in the New Testament were delivered via letters from the Apostle Paul to believers in the various Christian communities throughout the Roman Empire. These letters were a treasured form of communication for informing, encouraging, and—as we shall soon see—correcting these fledgling Christian communities. In this chapter we will hear the power of Paul's words spoken within the context of the early church in Corinth. We will hear Paul's words as Chloe might have heard them.

Chloe lived in Corinth and was one of the early members of the body of Christ. Concerned about struggles in her faith community, she sent a pleading word to move Paul to intervene. How do we know this? Paul tells us, mentioning in the letter he wrote to the Corinthian Christians, "For it has been reported to me by Chloe's people that there are quarrels among you, my brothers and sisters" (1 Cor. 1:11).

As was the tradition, Paul's letter was read aloud to the gathered community, so his words struck Chloe's ears and those of her quarreling brothers and sisters at the same time. Can you imagine the thoughts and feelings of those gathered to hear what Paul had to say to them? Do you wonder about the impact of Paul's words? Did God's Word delivered in Paul's words have the power to transform their lives and their life together?

Following is one interpretation of what listening to Paul's letter through the ears of Chloe might have sounded like. The story isn't created only from my imagination nor is it simply historical fact. Both imagination and history inform my reconstruction of the event and the effect that hearing the word of the cross proclaimed had on the community of believers in Corinth. I write not so much to inform you of the way it was, but to invite you to feel the force of the words in order that your community of faith might be transformed by the word of the cross.

What Chloe Heard

Chloe waits. Paul's messengers, Stephanas, Fortunatus and Achaicus, are due to arrive any minute. As she waits, she scans the familiar faces of the others in the room with her. Chloe wonders how many of them know that she has alerted Paul to the fact that there are divisions among them. She also wonders what they think of her because of it.

It was three years ago, Chloe remembers, that Paul first came to Corinth and gathered together a new community of believers through the Word of God proclaimed in his moving preaching. Being a part of this community is Chloe's greatest joy. The ways of this community are very different from the ways she knew growing up in the Roman world. She exercises leadership here. That surely wouldn't be possible in other circumstances. In fact, she marvels at how little the distinctions between men and women, Jew and Greek, slave and free matter in this community. *At least we say they don't matter*, she thinks as she watches people who have no status in the world outside of this little community of believers gather to hear what Paul has to say to them. Many are poor and live on the margins of society outside the circles of prestige and power. Yet in the community gathered in Christ's name, all are honored to be called God's beloved children.

But there are some who have come to hear Paul's letter who know honor in the outside world, too. They are greeted with approving nods of respect in the market place, and their words have power to set people into motion. They are movers and shakers in a world that is tailor-made for such people, and sometimes they forget that Christ has called them to an alternative way of living in a community vastly different from the proud city of Corinth.

In the best moments Chloe has seen how God's love moves these people of differing social backgrounds to love and honor each other. But lately, divisions have arisen among them, and the fault lines look all too familiar. Apollos[1] has his followers, she knows, but his influence is not always salutary! Chloe sees signs of the old way of living creeping into the community because of Apollos' influence. For example, the Lord's Supper—a meal of gracious remembrance—has become an opportunity for the wealthy to display their fine wines and luxurious food (1 Cor. 11). They use their expensive goods to embarrass those without such resources. She wonders what Paul will say about this. Can his words move the community she loves toward new life?

Now's the time to find out.

Achaicus steps into the room with Paul's letter in his hands. Stephanas and Fortunatus are with him, and all three men exchange greetings with their brothers and sisters in Christ. The room grows quiet when Achaicus raises his hand and, showing them the letter, announces that he brings word from Paul. People find places to sit so that they can listen as Achaicus reads. Chloe notices that they sit in cliques, largely according to personal means and social status. It's as though they have never heard the gospel! She also notes that some seem more eager for a word from Paul than others. Those with the least sit right at Achaicus' feet.

Achaicus has been coached well by Paul and he begins with greetings from the apostle. Chloe can almost hear Paul's voice and feel his presence as Achaicus proclaims, "To the church of God that is in Corinth, to those who are sanctified in Christ Jesus, called to be saints, together with all those who in every place call upon the name of our Lord Jesus Christ, both their Lord and ours: Grace to you and peace…" (1 Cor. 1:2, 3). Paul follows his greeting by giving thanks for the Corinthian believers. He is grateful that they are made strong in the Lord and he prays that Jesus might always be their strength. With the preliminaries over Paul wastes no time in getting to the reason for his letter: *There are quarrels among you!* Achaicus' voice rings out (1 Cor. 1:11, emphasis added).

Chloe looks down and takes a deep breath. She is aware of many eyes upon her as Achaicus reads her name, identifying her as the source of Paul's information. She had suspected that Paul would identify her, but that hadn't stopped her from contacting him. She was willing to take that risk in order to set things right within the community she loves.

Dispelling any notion that Paul had been misinformed about the quarrelling in Corinth, Achaicus continues reading, "What I mean is that each of you says, 'I belong to Paul.'" *What a smart move on Paul's part to refer to his leadership first,* Chloe thinks. "[Others say], 'I belong to Apollos,' or 'I belong to Cephas[2].'" People shift a bit in their seats and some stare at their feet when first Apollos and then Cephas are named. He notes that some even claim direct access to Christ, but Paul doesn't comment specifically about any of these allegiances. Instead he bombards the hearers with questions: "Has Christ been divided?" A few shake their heads. "Was Paul crucified for you?" This elicits audible denials. "Were you baptized in the name of Paul?" More head shaking. Chloe knows that some in the community were baptized by Paul, but certainly not *in his name* (1 Cor. 1:13).

Chloe is awed by how perfectly Paul has crafted his letter. Now that the people have begun to think twice about the allegiances that threaten to divide the community, Paul seizes the opportunity to talk about what unites them. He speaks of the unity they have in Christ alone. He admonishes them not to lean on wisdom that organizes the world into factions of "us" and "them" but to lean only on the cross of Christ and its strange power.

Strange indeed, Chloe thinks. Of all the elements of the new faith she embraces, this is the hardest to grasp. It makes no sense to her to say that God's glory and power are revealed in the death of God's Son. She understands enough about crucifixion to know that it is a shameful way to die and involves unimaginable suffering. She wonders, *Where is the glory in that? Cross and power—what a nonsensical combination of words!*

Paul knows what he's doing though. He has anticipated how frustrating it is to try to make sense of something that makes no sense: power revealed in weakness; glory in shame. Paul states it straight up: "The message of the cross is foolishness . . ." Achaicus delivers Paul's words perfectly. They hang in the air, teasing Chloe and allowing her to think for just a moment that she was right all along. But that's not the end of the sentence—thankfully! Achaicus reiterates, "The message of the cross is foolishness *to those who are perishing"* he pauses briefly, "but *to us who are being saved*, it is the power of God" (1 Cor. 1:18, emphasis added).

"[W]e proclaim Christ crucified, a stumbling block to Jews and foolishness to Gentiles, but to those who are the called, both Jews and Greeks, Christ the power of God and the wisdom of God" (1 Cor. 1:23, 24).

Why, that's us, Chloe thinks as she looks about the room where both Jew and Greek believers are gathered. *We are the called.* As if reading her mind, Achaicus smiles down at those sitting on the floor near him and glances up at a group in the corner before admonishing, "Consider your own call, brothers and sisters, not many [are] wise by human standards, not many [are] powerful, not many [are] of noble birth" (1 Cor. 1:26). Chloe notices that this seems to offend some in the room. They stir a bit, wondering, no doubt, where Paul is going.

Achaicus reads on, "But God chose what is foolish in the world to shame the wise; God chose what is weak in the world to shame the strong; God chose what is low and despised by the world, things that are not, to reduce to nothing things that are, so that no one might boast in the presence of God." *How well Paul knows us,* Chloe thinks. Not only are there quarrels among us, but there's a lot of boasting going on, too. Boasting that causes hurt and divides us further. "He is the source of your life in Christ Jesus, who became for us the wisdom of God, and righteousness and sanctification and redemption, in order that, as it is written, 'Let the one who boasts, *boast in the Lord'"* (1 Cor. 1: 27-31, emphasis added).

Achaicus stops. There is more, much more to read, but this is enough for now. He looks about the quiet room, so quiet, in fact, that you could hear an ant breathing. Chloe, too, looks about hoping to see some sign that Paul's words have had impact. The listeners begin to stir. She can tell that many are thinking hard about what they've heard.

Chloe ponders Paul's words until slowly it dawns on her that Paul has taken the cross of Christ—the instrument of his humiliation and death—and opened it up as a window into the ways of God. From this perspective status and power as defined by the world are flipped upside down. Suddenly she understands Paul's admonition that the message of the cross is foolishness to those who are perishing is intended for all who are tempted to buy into worldly values. Paul has pushed them to see the crucifixion of Jesus as a defining moment in the life of the community called in his name. He has demonstrated to those who look to power, prestige, and possessions to insulate them from others that they had best see themselves as perishing. Those who are being saved know to cling to the cross alone.

From the nervous glances passing between some of the believers, Chloe assumes that they, too, have figured out what Paul has done. It seems that his words have had immediate impact. Those who feel ashamed of their lack of education and whose family names do not matter in the marketplace have been lifted up by Paul's words connecting them to Jesus. Those who take for granted that they are wise and powerful feel deflated. They know shame in that moment—shame in realizing that their ways are not God's ways.

But will it make a difference, Chloe wonders. *The word of the cross puts us on common ground, but is it a word we're truly willing to hear? Are we ready to go where Christ would have us go? Are we ready to set aside the ways of the world and embrace the ways of God?* She watches closely as the believers gather their belongings. Wait. Is she imagining it, or are some with means looking with greater compassion on those who moments ago sat at Achaicus' feet?

Word of the Cross

In his letter to the church in Corinth, Paul challenged the premises on which the Corinthian believers arranged their lives and community. He then laid the essential groundwork for the believers in Corinth to deal with the many practical issues that grew out the divisions among them. Later in the letter he speaks of a leadership model that reflects the crucified Christ's option for the less honored (1 Corinthians 4) and expresses awareness of the weakness of his own flesh and blood, insisting that each one put aside arrogance and abuse of others. To the Corinthians, Paul emphasized celebrating the body of Christ without divisions. As a voice for the members of the body powerless to speak for themselves, he announced the need to honor all believers on the basis that all were called. Paul reminded the Corinthians of Christ's love that surpasses all and inspired hope that they would be raised one day even as God had already raised Jesus to new life.

Paul's words are timeless, calling first- and twenty-first-century believers who would prefer to live in spiritual high places back down to earth; reminding us that life in the body matters *now*. Paul proclaimed the word of the cross to remind the faithful of what is important, so, like Paul, we can proclaim by the way we live that "we have the mind of Christ" (1 Cor. 2:16).

The Gospel of Mark

Next we will hear the word of the cross from another source: the Gospel of Mark. Mark's Gospel is the oldest story of the life, death, and resurrection of Jesus that we possess. To ensure that the story continued to be told when eyewitnesses were no longer alive to tell it, the evangelist wrote it down, but not right away. After Jesus' death, over three decades passed before Mark put pen to paper. It takes time to work through the death of a loved one. Pain and grief are messy, and a generation is not too long a time to sort through such a tragedy. In fact, too quickly resolving grief into neat accounts may mean that things have been reflected on too lightly. We spend a lifetime resolving the loss of a mother to cancer, the traffic fatality of a friend, or the senseless, random murder of an acquaintance. Why should processing of the death of the one hoped to be *the* one happen any more quickly?

Before Mark's Gospel was recorded, the stories of Jesus' life, death, and resurrection passed from mouth to ear, from parent to child, from Jew to Gentile. Even afterward, the text served primarily to aid the continued oral proclamation of the story as the message was performed aloud in worship or educational contexts. Often it served as a prompt sheet for those who knew the story by heart, as it continues to do for storytellers today. In performing the gospel, storytellers exercise some flexibility in their presentations in order to meet the particular needs and challenges of the audience. The faithful embrace this fluidity, this possibility that Jesus does or says a new thing for a new time and place. After all, Jesus is risen, and he continues to speak in the life of the community.

The version of the gospel we call the Gospel of Mark was recorded in the wake of the Jewish War with Rome. For years the Romans inhabited the land of Jesus, controlling the lives of those who lived there. The people of Judea suffered a thousand indignities from the Romans daily. Tired of the constant occupation of their land by the Romans, the Jews revolted and tried to force the Romans out. Rome responded brutally. Josephus, an historian of the times, records that over a million Jews were killed, some by crucifixion. Due process mattered little, revolutionaries and ordinary people, men, women, and children were put to death. The heart of their religion was also destroyed; the Temple that symbolized God's special presence in the midst of Israel was demolished. Though this event happened well after the death of Jesus at Roman hands, this particular catastrophe loomed large for the storytellers and audiences who first shared Mark's Gospel. The storytellers asked what Jesus had to do with the particular wounds of their communities. The Gospel of Mark is one response. Even early on it's likely that Mark's Gospel was told in its entirety by storytellers who had committed it to memory. (Storytellers in our own day who have learned Mark's Gospel by heart can tell it in about two hours.) Imagine the impact of hearing such a dramatic story at an Easter baptismal service, when its intent is to remind the baptismal candidates of the way of life to which they are committing themselves. What follows is an imaginative reconstruction of the reflections of a baptismal candidate looking back at the story that he heard on the night of his baptism. How does the word of the cross, the story of Jesus' cross, shape the candidate's faith?

Remembering the Story

The storyteller had me from the moment he announced: "The beginning of the Good News of Jesus, the Christ, the Son of God" (Mark 1:1). *Yes*, I think, *this is it! This is how it all starts.* I realize that for him these words are simply a proclamation that he is about to tell the story of Jesus. But for me, on this night, the words speak of other beginnings that trace their beginnings to Jesus. The first is a movement that started with a small group of Jesus' followers and has continued to grow over the decades. I first learned about Jesus from these believers, and I became a believer because of them. But tonight I celebrate another beginning—the beginning of new life in Christ—for tonight I will be baptized. For me, this night the good news begins!

As if on cue, the storyteller begins with the story of Jesus' own baptism, revealing to me what Jesus saw in that event. Our eyes follow him as he looks up and describes how on that day the barriers between heaven and earth, between God and humanity were ripped apart before Jesus' eyes. As the storyteller scans the faces of the baptismal candidates, he speaks to us on God's behalf, echoing the words proclaimed from heaven on the day Jesus was baptized, "You are my beloved . . . , with you I am well pleased" (Mark 1:11).

In that moment Jesus was filled with the spirit of power and might! Yet this power is unlike that of the Romans who use their power to build themselves up, usually at our expense. By the power of the Spirit, Jesus empowers the down and out. He acts with compassion, healing the sick and freeing those occupied by demons. The storyteller brings us to synagogues, homes, and lakeshores. He shows us Jesus feeding the multitude and teaching them God's ways. For a moment, we are part of that crowd. We're caught up in the momentum of Jesus' ministry in Galilee; *immediately* going here, *immediately* going there, *immediately*, *immediately*, *immediately*. And everywhere Jesus heals. To think of Jesus as healer means a lot to me. I have watched infants die shortly after birth and witnessed the deaths of children who didn't even live ten years. Yes, my family knows sickness well. It is our constant companion. That Jesus brings healing is good news indeed.

But that's not all. Jesus also insists on going places he should not go. The storyteller says that Jesus made the disciples go to "the other side" again and again, and each time I know that he is crossing boundaries between Jewish lands of Galilee and those of the Gentiles on the other side of the sea. He cares for both without distinction.

Well, that is not quite true. We see a different picture in the story about a woman who comes to Jesus begging him to free her daughter from a demon. The woman is a Gentile—a Syro-Phoenician—and an enemy of the Jews. Up to this point Jesus has pretty much helped everyone who asked, but that isn't the case this time around. They have quite an exchange. Sparks fly, and, basically, Jesus calls her a dog. But she does not back down. She throws his words back in his face and he is moved. He commends her for her faith. In the end the woman's child is healed by Jesus, and Jesus is changed by his encounter with the woman (Mark 7:24-30). This becomes evident a little while later when the storyteller tells us that Jesus multiplies bread "on the other side" to feed to a multitude of Gentiles (Mark 8:1-10) just as he had done earlier with his own people (Mark 6:30-44).

It is striking, even a bit disconcerting to see Jesus mature in his understanding of God's will; to see his horizons broaden. I suppose he will ask me to stretch my horizons, too. Shall I look again at how I treat my enemies? He may be taking me places I'm not quite ready to go! It wouldn't be the first time he's done that.

In the middle of the story, Jesus leaves the Galilee of his feedings and healings and turns toward Jerusalem in all her glory. This, of course, is before the Romans destroyed our capital and scattered us throughout the land. As Jesus moves out of Galilee and toward Jerusalem, he tries to bring his followers along with him—in more ways than one. But they don't get it. Jesus says he has to go to Jerusalem where he will be crucified, but Peter tries to turn him back by suggesting it would be better to live as a healer in Galilee than die in Jerusalem (Mark 8:32). Of course all Jesus' talk of the cross is puzzling for them. I understand that. As one who has witnessed the crucifixions of many people I care about, mere mention of a cross fills me with rage. How could Jesus' disciples have understood what Jesus meant if, three decades later, I still struggle to understand? But, clearly, facing the cross meant something to Jesus. And from what I can tell it had to do with his desire to live out his teaching and embody a new way of being in the world.

On the journey to Jerusalem, Jesus' followers seem to fixate on a desire for power. Anticipating a worldly kingdom, they argue about who will get the seats of honor when Jesus comes to power (Mark 9:34). But Jesus has none of this. As the men circle around Jesus asking who is the greatest, Jesus breaks through the circle and puts a little girl in their midst, as if to say, "You want to be great then do not seek to dominate. In the new community that God is creating, the child, that is the one who is least among you, the one who is most vulnerable, must be at the center. If you want to be great, then look after these little ones." I can tell you that in my world children do not count for much, but according to Jesus, God's new community belongs precisely to such people. I cannot emphasize enough how much this way of living upends everything we have been taught.

In the end, it is this commitment to look after the vulnerable and to stand up to those who wish them harm that leads to Jesus' death on the cross. His death is the price paid for the life he lived. Even if he had stayed in Galilee, he would have met with a violent death eventually. I'm sure of it because in this world, people who love like Jesus don't live long. Jesus was not the first nor will he be the last to die at the power-thirsty hands of Rome. In fact, the storyteller tells us of another, Rome condemned to die—a revolutionary named Barabbas (Mark 15:6-16). I find it interesting that both Jesus and Barabbas resist Roman tyranny. Both long for a world in which God's will rather than Caesar's is done. Jesus chooses a way of transformation without violence, refusing to resort to a kind of power that depends on destruction and death to get its way in the world. Barabbas, on the other hand, tries to reclaim our land with the occupier's own weapons. He chooses the road of violence, and, sadly, many of my people follow him. In fact, the storyteller relates that when given the choice between freeing Jesus, the healer, or Barabbas, the murderer, shouts of "Barabbas! Barabbas!" fill the air.

I wonder how it might have been different if my people had called for Jesus' release instead, What if we had chosen to walk in the ways of Jesus? Would the Temple still stand? Would my brother Jeremiah and my sisters Hannah and Miriam still live? I don't know the answers to these questions. Perhaps I seek answers where there are none, but beneath these questions loom others I'm afraid to ask: Did God abandon us? Did we abandon God?

The storyteller has reached the point in the story where Jesus is led away to be scourged before being hoisted aloft on a cross to die the slow death of suffocation. As he relates the events of Jesus' passion I am suddenly caught off guard by grief—immense grief that I try to hide because it is too painful to face. As the storyteller weaves the story of Jesus' brutal death, I am overwhelmed with a fresh sense of all that I have lost: family, friends, home, land, Temple, even Jerusalem—the holy city. All the destruction and the pointless deaths I have witnessed converge in the story of Jesus' death. Grief flows into grief until I can hold back the tears no longer. I am bereft. Jesus' cry from the cross—*My God, my God, why have you abandoned me?*—becomes my cry (Mark 15:34). My anguish is so great that it takes all my strength to keep from crying the words aloud, demanding that God answer me.

And then something miraculous happens. In my mind's eye I see Jesus hanging on the cross even as I hear the words *this is my beloved Son—listen to him* whispered in my ear. In that instant I am viscerally aware of God's presence and I realize that in Jesus God knows my pain and the pain of my people. God knows the humiliation we suffer. In Jesus God knows what it is like to be abandoned in time of great need. God knows the bitterness of death, especially the bitterness of dying alone with no one to stand up for you. *This is my beloved Son. Listen to him.* It occurs to me that on this night when I am about to be baptized in Jesus' name, God is preparing me to be attentive to the cries of others, reminding me that these, too, are God's beloved. *Listen to him. Walk in his ways, trusting in the power of love; refusing to give into fear.*

With these words ringing in my ears, I move forward to be baptized. My senses come alive as I step into the cool water. Firm hands plunge my face beneath the surface, drowning my old life with all its sins and sorrows. I gulp for air and in that moment I am born anew into life with Christ Jesus. From this moment on I vow to proclaim Christ only, and him crucified.

* * * * *

I should note that tonight's story raises as many questions as it provides answers. I've heard stories of Jesus visiting people after his resurrection, but the storyteller neglects to mention these. He relates that some of the women who followed Jesus went to the tomb on the morning after his crucifixion in order to anoint his body. They find the tomb empty and a young man in white robes sits where Jesus' body had been. He tells them that Jesus is raised and has gone ahead of them to Galilee, promising to meet them there. "So they went out and fled from the tomb, for terror and amazement had seized them," the storyteller announces, "and they said nothing to anyone, for they were afraid" (Mark 16:8).[3]

I want to scream, *what kind of ending is that?*

Talk about questions without answers! Where is Jesus? How do we know that he will meet us in Galilee? How can the women keep this announcement to themselves? If they kept it to themselves, how is it that we know the story?

Still wearing my white baptismal robe, I walk over to the storyteller. *Why end it like this?* I ask. *Surely you know the other stories. You could have finished the story for us!*

He smiles at me and says, "I do know of other endings, but this one seems right to me. I personally have never touched the risen Christ. That may have been the pleasure of another generation, but the privilege has been denied to me. I believe we live our lives in faith, not certainty. We live caught between the cry of abandonment and the promise of risen life. It is a precarious place, but it is the only one I know.

"I have come to believe that absolute certainty leads to arrogance and arrogance leads to violence. When we feel like we possess the truth, even the truth of God's just cause and merciful nature, we use that certainty in unjust ways devoid of mercy. You may have noticed that no one in my story possesses all truth. Even Jesus had to learn from his enemies. Did you hear what he learned from the Syro-Phoenician woman? Did you notice that even while grieving the execution of his Son, God inspired faith in the one who was complicit in that execution? (Mark 15:38-39) If the enemy who pounded the nails into Jesus' hands could come around to see who he truly was, then how shall we treat those opposed to us? Can we help our enemies to see the deadliness they deliver so they seek a more excellent way?

"Do you notice that all who are certain in this storytelling end as certainly wrong. Beware of certainty when it aligns with power. I cannot offer you certainty, but I do offer you a promise from one who is certainly trustworthy. He will meet you in Galilee. He will meet you when you walk in his way—trusting in God, feeding the hungry, freeing the captives, crossing the boundaries between 'us' and 'them,' loving your enemies, tending to the vulnerable ones. I cannot offer you certainty, but I do offer you faith. And for this night, perhaps that will do."

* * * * *

On this night I was baptized. I was brought into Christ's death and I now find myself like the young man dressed in white who points the women toward Galilee; I am ready to trust in the risen one. I still know the suffering I have seen, but I know that we are not alone in this, that God shares in our suffering in ways I am only beginning to glimpse. As my people said of old, the LORD has seen our oppression, has heard our cries, knows our sufferings from within, but has come down to help (Ex. 3:7-8). I pray that I might learn to walk courageously with God in faith into Galilee and beyond the horizon to wherever he leads me.

For Further Thought

1. In this day and age when words come to us increasingly in the spoken rather than written form, what difference does it make to you to hear words rather than read them? Is there an instance when hearing words had an immediate effect on you?

2. What insights regarding the Word of the Cross did you gain from this chapter?

3. How does your church equip you to exchange worldly glory with its emphasis on power, prestige, and possessions for that offered in Jesus' death and resurrection?

4. What surprises you in the baptismal candidate's witness to the word? How does hearing this word in its original context deepen your understanding of it?

5. What do you think that the Word of the Cross reveals to us about God?

*For by grace you have been saved through faith, and this is
not your own doing; it is the gift of God—*

Ephesians 2:8

2

The Word of the Cross in Reformation Germany

In the sixteenth century a German monk who believed God to be a wrathful God discovered something very different in the pages of the Bible. Martin Luther's intense wrestling with Scripture blessed him with a new understanding of God, an understanding that turned his world upside down. Focusing on the word brought by Jesus hanging upon the cross and then raised by God, Luther came to see that the righteousness of God is not a human achievement but is God's gift to humanity in Christ. This word of the cross invited him to simple trust in the God who graciously claimed him. The Law with all its demands and its attacks upon his soul no longer prevailed. Luther held tight to a promise that makes all things new! In Jesus, God declares righteous even those who are enemies of God. The free gift of God's salvation became the starting point for rethinking everything Luther thought he knew. His theology of the cross grew out of rich, biblical soil. He saw the cross as a critique of a church that tried to sell heavenly glory for a couple of copper coins. Luther proclaimed the word of the cross day in and day out, trusting that such a word can change the world.

The printing press undoubtedly helped the gospel move beyond Wittenberg, but Luther held that true power was found in the proclaimed and heard word. He had good reason to believe this since ninety-nine percent of the population in Luther's Germany couldn't read and the vast majority of the people received the gospel and Luther's insights into it by word of mouth. The communication process likely looked something like this: Luther wrote a piece that was then printed by a local printer. It was read by a parish priest who then preached the whole piece or reworked it to conform better to his purposes. Those who heard the message preached, carried it into the marketplace, interpreting it a bit in the sharing of it. Then a new hearer of the word, a merchant, perhaps, repeated what he heard to those who gathered in the tavern at the end of the day. And so the word was dynamic.

This complex process is a lot messier than what is communicated in the uniform type of the printed page, but the spread itself is more interesting. About one quarter of urban community members in Luther's day were domestic servants, and an even larger percentage were former domestics with just enough money to live a bit more independently. They lived under the watchful eyes of their employers with little life of their own until they were able to marry. What might ordinary people have taken from Luther's message? How did conversations about the word of the cross, interpreted by Luther go between ordinary folks? In answer I offer the following series of conversations between servants in a bishop's household during Luther's time. The main characters, Marie and Hans, encounter Luther's message in various ways. His works affect their daily lives subtly yet dramatically. Each dialogue between Marie and Hans is preceded by a brief introduction to the writing that inspired the rumors they discuss.[1]

About the Ninety-five Theses

The Reformation first thrust itself on the stage of history in 1517 when Luther wrote the Ninety-five Theses.[2] Luther argues against the practice of paying the church a fee to send loved ones through the glorious gates of heaven. These arguments against the practice of indulgences began as an academic debate, found their way into the lives of the German people, and struck a spark that changed the world. Here Hans and Marie discuss Luther's message as it has been filtered to them through the man for whom they work. The bishop's displeasure with Luther's message intrigues them.

Conversation One

HANS: Well, the master is out of sorts this evening. He nearly bit my head off when he came in tonight.

MARIE: Seems he read something that didn't meet his approval.

HANS: What might that have been?

MARIE: It appears someone has attacked his precious indulgences. You know how the master counts on that money for his projects. Well, a monk has attacked the practice as unchristian.

HANS: Really? Upon what grounds?

MARIE: I wasn't there, but I heard the master grumbling to his friend, "We sell indulgences for the sake of those people's souls. How dare he say we are just out for money! Why, he dared to challenge the pope himself, saying he should forgive the sins of the rabble *gratis*, for free! Does he really think they would appreciate that? A free gift isn't properly appreciated! People have to work for something to know its value."

HANS: I have heard that comment before. Always struck me as a bit odd that he—with his feet up on the table and you feeding him a feast—should reprimand others for not working.

MARIE: Especially since *you* have already put in several hours of work by the time he makes it to breakfast.

HANS: Got that right. Go on, what else is troubling the master?

MARIE: He muttered something about the monk's claim that God is being presented as a businessman out to make a profit. Well, the good bishop didn't understand how that monk could see this as a problem. He complained, "Businessmen just use that which God has given them! They even loan to those in need. "If God is like them, it is because the people God helps don't appreciate him, just like here in Germany the people bark at the ones that feed them."

HANS: That's the master's voice all right. My take is a bit different than his. My uncle tried to move his family ahead by borrowing money from one of those who were "blessed by God." It wasn't his business that grew but his debt. My uncle is more broke now than he ever was and five times as frustrated. Seems to me the master has money invested in this practice, too. Do you think that might be shaping his opinion?

MARIE: Without a doubt! Oh, the final blow according to the master is that this monk wishes to limit the power of the pope.

HANS: Are you sure that he is a monk? Doesn't much sound like a thing a monk would wish to do. Most I know are looking to get more power, not to mention coins, into the hands of the pope.

MARIE: He is a monk all right, an Augustinian. And I say with him, the pope could use some limiting. He is bleeding our poor Germany dry to build up his Rome.

HANS: Building up that and the money in the pope's bank vault, not to mention the pocket of our dear employer. Well, saints be praised! When a monk can see what we have known all along and even say it out loud for once, maybe there is hope for us after all.

MARIE: Maybe it's even worth bearing the master's bad temper. This monk apparently wants to teach the master something about the cross. The master thought that was rich! "Like I don't know the meaning of the cross," he grumbled. Well, hopefully something good will come out of all this. I'd best go. He'll be wanting his dinner soon.

HANS: Until later, love.

About the *Heidelberg Disputation*

Shortly after the publishing of the Ninety-five Theses, Luther was invited to another debate, this time in Heidelberg.[3] No other document has shaped the Lutheran interpretation of the theology of the cross as significantly as the *Heidelberg Disputation* in which Luther speaks of the theology of the cross in terms of God being present in suffering and the cross. Luther criticizes theologians of glory who use God in order to protect their own privilege. They believe they have special access to God and then use that claim to run over anyone who stands in their way. They use God's Law to puff themselves up and to deal death to others. Luther complains that such people possess volatile knowledge, that is, knowledge prone to violence.

Conversation Two

HANS: Has the master returned from Heidelberg yet?

MARIE: You haven't heard the screams! He is back and aggravated. The master had his friend with him for lunch and spent his whole meal raving about that monk Luther again.

HANS: Tell me more; I'm interested.

MARIE: He said that the idiot is undermining everything that was most beautiful and precious. The master spews insult after insult. The beer Luther devours has him drunk as a skunk. . . . Luther wants to pull down centuries of great thinkers. . . . Luther doesn't understand the importance of the law and is just bitter because he couldn't make it in law school. . . . Luther wants our work to be done for us so we can rest in God's love and faithfulness alone.

HANS: Ah, the more the master rants against Luther, the more I find myself drawn to that strange monk. He is for beer and against the law and labor. What's not to like? The law has been no friend to me. It only shows up at my door to punish, never to protect. The law serves them that have money in their pockets. And it fills their pockets even more. But what chance has a poor soul like me got in front of the law? If Luther couldn't be a lawyer, maybe it is because he is inclined to call things what they are.

MARIE: Of course, the master doesn't see things that way. He said Luther is a German fool and how could you expect a German to know anything about theology? He said Luther wants us to listen to the people's groans, to listen to the common people's hopes. His friend said, "What a great idea! Let's put the poor and destitute in the pulpit." The master didn't know I was listening. He said to his friend, "Shall I invite Marie in and have her teach us about God?!" They had a good laugh about that one.

HANS: But that you could, Marie. Your faith in God may be simple, but it is pure. I suspect buried under all that greed of his, master has some faith in God, but darned if I can see it.

MARIE: And him a servant of God!

HANS: Or of the devil!

MARIE: Apparently Luther says that the master and his cohorts are looking in all the wrong places for God. They are looking at all that shines of gold . . .

HANS: German gold, if I'm not mistaken.

MARIE: . . . and refuse to look at the poor man Jesus hanging on the cross.

HANS: You have a crucifix hanging in your room, Marie. Jesus and his Blessed Mother, too. They are not gazing at the gold, trying to figure out how to wring more from our German hides. They know pain—pain like yours and mine, Marie.

MARIE: Exactly the monk's point, I believe. The master doesn't quite see it that way. He only looks to us to polish Mary's crown so that he can trick the people into thinking he speaks on her behalf. He knows nothing of the wounds and suffering of Jesus. He knows nothing about our suffering either.

HANS: I wish I could read. I'd like to learn more about this monk who thinks that he could learn from us.

MARIE: I am afraid he won't be around for long. The master said he will be silenced soon enough. With rage in his eyes, the master muttered, "We shall show him the power of what we know!" And then he and his friend laughed viciously. I best be going, he'll be looking for me about now.

HANS: To fill his ear with your wisdom about God.

MARIE: More to fill his belly and cup.

About *The Blessed Sacrament of the Holy and True Body of Christ and the Brotherhoods*

In 1519 Luther wrote three sermons that proclaimed in basic language the power conveyed by baptism, the Lord's Supper, and the forgiveness of sins. The sermon on the Lord's Supper was entitled *The Blessed Sacrament of the Holy and True Body of Christ and the Brotherhoods.*[4] In it Luther describes the Lord's Supper as a meal through which Christ participates in his people's suffering so that they will share and support each other in the same way.

Conversation Three

MARIE: Hans, I finally got to hear the words of Luther without the interference of the master's interpretation.

HANS: Where was he that you heard him?

MARIE: Well, I didn't actually hear him, but I did hear someone reading one of his sermons at the market. It was quite interesting.

HANS: Do tell.

MARIE: It was a sermon on the true body and blood at the Lord's Supper. It was really lovely. He spoke of the true meaning of being the church. God isn't as tied to the priests—and only the priests—as they would have us believe. The whole point of the sermon was that everyone in the community of faith matters.

HANS: Because some pay for the church and others benefit from it?

MARIE: You know Luther wouldn't say that. In fact, he says that those who are only out looking for their own benefit, benefit nothing from this sacrament. He says that in the sacrament God transforms us into a new body. We live trusting in God and loving one another. We are kind of stuck with each other when we hold onto God's gifts.

HANS: And you like that idea?

MARIE: Yes, because like it or not, you and I seem to be stuck with the master. We have to do his bidding. But Luther speaks of a different way of being connected together. He says that Christ and all the saints serve those who have great needs. And when he talks about saints, he means you and me.

HANS: I've always thought you were a saint, Marie, but I'm not so convinced in my own case.

MARIE: Luther is convinced of such. Not because you are such a great person but because God is so great and loving. God doesn't ask us to do super acts of goodness. God invites us to trust in the divine promise and see the neighbor who is in need. Luther said we are like a body. When you, Hans, are out in the garden and drop a rock on your foot, what happens? Your eyes race to inspect your foot, your hands rush to cradle it, your other foot holds your weight as you hop about and your mouth cries out so that the whole world knows this is not a desirable state of affairs. Well, Luther wants the church to be like that; everyone rushing to the aid of the member who suffers.

HANS: That would be a switch. Usually my experience of church is the rock dropping part with all its pain. I am beginning to believe that Luther may be the voice you speak of. He's screaming bloody murder for the pain that has been caused us.

MARIE: Luther's voice is worth hearing. He says Christ on the cross was God coming to heal our wounds. Jesus holds onto us unashamed of being joined to us. He takes our suffering and he gives us his blessedness. If Jesus stands with me like that then I have the strength to stand with you. Luther helps me to hear not only his own voice but that of God and of my neighbors as well. I like the idea that the church is not all in Rome nor is the priest the whole of the church, but that God is making us into a body where every part matters, has its role, is bound to all the others.

HANS: I have an idea which part the master must be!

About Luther's Commentary on the Magnificat

In 1521 Luther wrote a lovely reflection on Mary's song from the second chapter of Luke's Gospel.[5] He wrote it in German and sent a large part of it to the printers in front of his trial before the Diet at Worms where Luther was called to renounce his *Ninety-Five Theses* and other of his writings criticizing the Church. In the conversation that follows, Hans tells Marie about this commentary in which Luther depicts the mother of Jesus as a domestic servant, like Marie herself.

Conversation Four

HANS: Marie, it was my turn to come across the work of Luther! The boy training to be a printer shared with me something that Luther has been working on.

MARIE: I think by now it is everybody's turn to come across what Luther does! The printers jump to sell anything that comes from his pen, and his pen never stops! He keeps writing and writing about divine mercy.

HANS: Well, I suppose that is the theme of this work in progress that was read to me. Luther is reflecting on the song that Jesus' mother Mary sang when she found out she'd be bearing the Christ child.

MARIE: The song of the Queen of Heaven—that is a good theme! Now there is a woman who is ready to listen to my cries. Bless her!

HANS: Luther's point was that she is closer to you than you think, not as Queen of Heaven, but as a woman just like yourself, Marie.

MARIE: I don't follow you.

HANS: Luther says Mary was a woman just like you: a domestic servant in the house of rich man. No one who saw her would have thought to call her a Queen, if they noticed her at all.

MARIE: Then why would God choose her? I mean, God could choose anyone.

HANS: According to Luther, God chose her because . . . well that is just the way God does things. God's faithfulness is always offered to them that everyone else overlooks. Mary isn't an exception to the rule; that is the way that God rules the world—picking the ones who are poor and disrespected by the likes of the master, and making of them leaders in his kingdom. Jesus revealed God in the dishonor of the cross. God always appears among the lowly.

MARIE: There is nothing about Mary that draws God's eye toward her, say, her obedience or humility?

HANS: God chooses her because those who are nothing to others are very special for him. If Mary had a virtue it was that she didn't look down on other servant girls but rather looked on them as God's own children. But really God is the key. God's word makes Mary trust in God's promise to her. God's word brings Mary to faith and raises her up. God always and only looks at those who are nothing, despised, overworked, and underpaid by the powerful of the world. They are at the center of God's kingdom.

MARIE: Then God might as well choose you and me, Hans!

HANS: That is Luther's point! God looks with love upon you and me and chooses us to lead the world into a new way of seeing and being. God sees what the powerful ignore; God respects what they disrespect; God looks at what they overlook! And when we trust that God respects us, we come to respect ourselves in new ways. We trust that God is our God and will do great things for us.

MARIE: I think the master won't love this much.

HANS: Luther has a word for him too! He says that as much as the Holy Scriptures bring good news to domestics like us, what they say to the powerful is a warning to change their ways. "The word constrains them to fear," he says.

MARIE: The man is turning everything upside down!

HANS: God is turning everything upside down. Don't you remember Mary's song to God? It goes something like this. "God, you have taken the powerful from their thrones and put in their place those who are nothing. You have fed the hungry with a great feast and sent away empty those who are used to being served."[6]

MARIE: That turns *everything* around . . . yet it is a song I would love to sing.

HANS: Then sing with faith, woman! God is looking upon you! Sing, trust, sing! Bear the Christ into the world!

About "The Passion of the Christ and of the Antichrist"

Marie and Hans's final conversation is about a work that is more visual than verbal. In 1521 Luther, together with the artist Lucas Cranach the Elder and, perhaps, Luther's good friend Philip Melancthon, put together a series of twenty-six images contrasting the life of Jesus with that of the pope. The title offers commentary enough; they called it "The Passion of the Christ and of the Antichrist."[7]

Conversation Five

MARIE: Hans, look what I got at the market place—a pamphlet on themes from Martin Luther. Look, it is filled with pictures so that we can read it for ourselves.

HANS: What is this called?

MARIE: "The Passion of Christ and the Antichrist." You can tell quite quickly who is the Antichrist! The Holy Father doesn't come off very well in this piece.

HANS: What a riot! It sure does tell it like it is. There is Jesus seeking out people who need his help and there is the pope getting fat on his privileges!

MARIE: What strikes me is all the weapons the pope has on his side! He is not going to let privilege slip through his fingers.

HANS: He has a lot to protect. See, tracks of land, huge parties, and German coins. I guess we shouldn't need a pamphlet to have us see this. These could practically be scenes of daily life in Germany, if the pope actually showed up to be with us.

MARIE: That is a good point. Look at these pictures. Where do you see us, Hans? Where are we in all this mess?

HANS: Once I might have said, paying the pope his dues. That wouldn't be a lie, mind you. But I am coming to see that this is not the whole story. These pictures help me put it all together in my mind.

MARIE: How is that?

HANS: The church has spent many a day caring for itself instead of caring for the poor. We might be the ones paying the pope's dues or losing our land to him. We might be the servants in the party. But that isn't the whole story. Look at these other pictures, too. They show us how Jesus treats the people. They show us what God thinks of the present state of the church.

MARIE: That is clear in this one where the pope goes to hell!

HANS: Yes, but it is also clear that if Jesus is God then God is living among us with love. And while the laws of the pope take advantage of us, God frees us. God stands by our side and doesn't abandon us.

MARIE: That is lovely. While some wound us, God seeks our healing, like Jesus is doing in this picture right here. I could imagine this fellow going to market with me to buy the master's food.

HANS: While the pope and his crowd are strutting around with swords and cannons, Jesus is walking around with the rest of us, showing God's love and justice.

MARIE: While some bleed us dry, God is willing to suffer our kind of suffering. Look at this crown they are forcing on Jesus' head!

HANS: Thorns!

MARIE: A crown of thorns!

HANS: If God stands with us, Marie . . .

MARIE: . . . then who could stand against us?

HANS: Amen. Better put those pictures away where the master won't see them.

> **MARIE:** Don't you think it would make nice breakfast reading for him?
>
> **HANS:** Tuck it away. I don't think he'd see the grace in it.

Concluding Thoughts

Hans and Marie have helped us see that Luther's words addressed real people caught in major imbalances of power, helping them understand the word of the cross in light of their own life situations. Together with Luther the common people came to understand that the one who was crucified upon the cross meets them in everyday life, in the very places where they are condemned and beaten down. Luther communicated in concrete ways that the God revealed in Jesus is *for* them. In a world radically divided between those who trusted in their own wealth and power and those who knew the harshness of their own poverty, God chose to act in a new way, siding with those whom the powerful inevitably ignore.

In the conversations between Hans and Marie, we have seen that God looks with favor upon those who are weak. God's gracious gaze upon those deemed unsightly by the world is pure gift to them! They are raised up into a new reality above all that beats them down. The glory of God is respect for the disrespected. The word of the cross is assurance that God is trustworthy, and trusting in God is life-transforming.

For Further Thought

1. What connections do you see between the way the Corinthians heard the word of the cross and the way that Marie and Hans heard it?

2. When does your own church use its power ungraciously? Who are the people ignored or abused?

3. Go to the Richard C. Kessler Reformation Collection on the Pitts Theology library Web site http://www.pitts.emory.edu/dia/1521LuthWWBook/pc1.cfm and look at the pamphlet that Hans and Marie discussed. What do you notice in it?

For I am convinced that neither death, nor life, nor angels, nor rulers, nor things present, nor things to come, nor powers, nor height, nor depth, nor anything else in all creation, will be able to separate us from the love of God in Christ Jesus our Lord.

Romans 8:38-39

3

The Word of the Cross in Middle America: My Story

My Family

I first heard the word of the cross in a small town called Menominee in the Upper Peninsula of Michigan. Yet well before I heard that gracious word, events came together that set the stage for my experience of the gospel.

My father grew up in a church where every message started with the word *NO*. The pastors sought to shape people up by driving home the law of God with proclamations like, "No attending movies, no dancing, no drinking." Laws defined one's relationship with God. My father was an active boy in the days before we started medicating our children to control their behavior. So he heard many *NOs* in his life that reinforced his church's message. Eventually, he had enough and left the church.

My mother's life followed a different course. Early on she was badly burned when playing with fireworks. She spent long months in bed as she waited for the scars that covered her torso to heal. When she returned to school, well-meaning teachers warned her friends to be gentle around Lola lest she be injured again. As a result, she was often left alone. Yet a sense of wholeness and compassion grew within her scarred body. Rooted in the message of grace that her Lutheran church proclaimed, Lola became a gracious and loving person.

Over a decade after my father left the church, he and my mother met on a blind date. Though my father was stationed in Washington, D.C., and my mother lived in Wisconsin, they fell in love through a handful of dates and months of daily letters. My father speaks often of the transforming power of my mother's unconditional love for him— love rooted in and shaped by God's love. My anti-church father was so moved by this love, he set out for college so that he could go on to seminary and eventually be ordained. From a variety of church pulpits, my father spent nearly half a century announcing to others God's word of unconditional love.

God's love still comes through my mother's patient dedication and attention to everyone she meets. My father's mission in life to love people where they are at is shaped by his own experience of grace. Countless people have been inspired by the love my parents share. Mom and Dad know each other's rhythms and turns. Like many long-time companions, they move together as one even in their differences. Their graceful dance of over five decades has left the world a more beautiful place. Even before I was formed in my mother's womb, my parent's love was preparing the soil for gospel proclamation in my life.

My Growing-Up Church

I first encountered the word of the cross through the love of my parents, but that word touched me in other situations as well. I recall gathering in a musty basement of the old parish hall of Emmanuel Lutheran Church and making crosses out of Popsicle sticks under the guidance of Tena Magnuson. Tena put wheels on my early faith through her faithful Sunday school teaching. (She much later gave me the car she could no longer drive, a '66 Olds with three-in-the-tree standard transmission.) And there was John Helfert, my scoutmaster, who wrote songs that our church youth choir sang. When I ran into him some thirty years later, I was pleasantly surprised to discover that I still carried in my heart the lyrics to a song he composed about supporting each other through mutual prayer. I also remember Paul Anderson, our first intern at Emmanuel, who showed me that a Christian could be a little bit crazy and fun to be with. These are but a few members of the community of faith who crossed my path with grace. From the beginning of my life, God's word of grace was enfleshed in people like Tena, John, and Paul.

Their flesh, like that of my mother, was not without its scars. Yet in them was life! They taught me that there is no place in my world where I would be separated from God's love.

Reflecting on Emmanuel's Word of the Cross

What then was the word that shaped our community of faith? In Jesus Christ God comes to be among us. God is not a distant, demanding deity but one who puts on a servant's apron and comes down to be with us. In Jesus Christ the world experiences God's activity making all things new. God stoops to embrace us, reclaiming his wayward creation. Jesus reveals the heart of God as love toward creation, toward you and me. Jesus comes to claim the whole of our lives, not only what is beautiful and glorious in us, but also what is weak, condemned, and shattered. He claims our whole heart, soul, mind, and strength, knowing full well that those hearts are often broken hearts; understanding that our souls are profoundly messed up; realizing that our minds are frequently confused; that our strength is often depleted or focused in the wrong direction. In Jesus Christ, God's word to us is not the *NO!* of my father's childhood church, but a full, hearty, and divine *YES!* This total gift of God promises me and all creation a new identity that is grounded in the source of all that exists! In the presence of such an outrageous gift, believers are not defined by the law and its demands but by the gospel and its freedom. In this freedom we turn to our neighbors so we might serve them.

A Story Worth Entering

The story of God's extravagant love moves the hearers of that story out into the world, transformed by that love. In the community of Emmanuel Lutheran Church, I found this word of love and it became my home. The story of God's love for God's people witnessed to in the Scriptures became a dwelling place of grace within which my personal story made sense. In Scripture's multifaceted witness I discovered the God who made and calls all of creation good, very good. I learned of

God's plan to bless the world through a particular man and woman, old Abraham and barren Sarah. I took notice of how God heard the cries of a people trapped in slavery and, seeing their suffering, came down to free them. The word invited me to travel through the wilderness with those people, who even when they forgot God, were not forgotten by God. I learned of the God who found a place for that rambling band of people so that they could live together in the freedom they had been denied in Egypt. I listened as God spoke to them through the prophets to bring them back to freedom from new kinds of enslavement. I watched as God's people were dragged into exile and learned that God suffered exile with them in order to bring them home again. Each time the divine promise was renewed, the divine promise renewed people.

And I was shown that in Jesus Christ, the God of Abraham and Sarah, Moses and Miriam, the prophets, and the forgotten responded to new cries and sufferings. I put on a tinsel halo and my father's t-shirt, and sang with angels of the wonder of Emmanuel, *God with us*. Jesus came offering healing to the broken, casting out demons from the possessed, preaching good news to the desperate, and breaking down walls of hostility. Jesus announced the forgiveness of God for sinners like us. As he suffered the fate of sinners, I sang of being there—"tremble, tremble." I heard him cry out so humanly, "My God, my God, why have you forsaken me?" I watched from a distance with the women as he breathed his last, and I also sang *Alleluia*! when the crucified and risen one showed us his scars. As he offered us his peace in the face of grief, guilt, betrayal, fear, and doubt, I was lifted into a new place where death has lost its sting. And I leaned into the promise that God will wipe away my grandfather's tears and I will join him one day when God is all in all.

The Flip Side of the Story Worth Entering

Don't get the idea that the only word at Emmanuel was *grace*, that freedom was the only reality. Other words invaded, speaking not hope but despair: *divorce, cancer, stillborn, drunk, rape, doubt, sin, rejection, failure*. Such words of brokenness tried to seize divine turf and define us. The message of God's grace is not something that we need hear only once; it must sound in our ears again and again. Our money, our "stuff," our relatively decent lives cannot protect us from pain, loss, guilt, and death.

Even as a child I knew when God's law struck my heart telling me I had screwed up. I recall an instance when I promised my dad that I would help him with a vacation Bible school activity that only I could lead. But when the time came my mind was on other things and I forgot all about it. Later, when I saw Dad and realized that I had left him stranded, the look on his face immediately filled me with a sense of guilt for being selfish and irresponsible. But in response to my betrayal, my father offered a word of grace. True, I had screwed up, but that wasn't how the story ended. At that moment and many times since, my father forgave me and the God who raised Jesus from the dead lifted me up from where I had fallen and provided me the opportunity to begin again to live as God's beloved child. I learned then that the glory of God is the embraced and forgiven sinner.

My friend Ray Picket is a biblical scholar and all-around fine human being. He reads the gospel daily in the original Greek. He also thinks with greater care than most of us about the way that our culture tries to define us on its own terms.

When Ray's daughter showed signs of being an Olympic hopeful, he found a local swim coach experienced in training medalists to work with her. The lessons took place at a local country club, which was very unfamiliar territory for a humble seminary professor with an old beater of a car. Nevertheless, each week Ray drove into that haven for Mercedes and BMWs to deliver his aspiring Olympic athlete to lessons only to feel himself diminished amidst all the other symbols of wealth and prestige in the country club parking lot. "The American advertising machine would have us believe that we are what we drive," Ray once told me. "I know better than that! I know that my worth is in no way related to the sticker price of my vehicle. Yet I cringe every time I drive into the parking lot. I mean, if you are what you drive, what does that mean if you are driving a piece of junk?"

Even the strongest of us feel judged according to the standards of a consumer culture, a standard that we can never live up to. No wonder then that we yearn desperately for a word of grace by which to be defined and claimed as God's own.

When you enter my home, the first thing you see is a ceramic plaque announcing, "I cleaned my house yesterday . . . wish you could have seen it." My wife was pastor of a congregation when our daughter was young so I stayed home with her during the day. Many days I would work my way across the living room, bringing order to the toy-strewn space, only to get to the other end of the room and see the wake of reconstituted chaos behind me. I could have despaired of the time and energy wasted, but I knew that had I chosen to ignore the mess in the first place, ultimately the teddy bears and building blocks would have taken over the space. The word of the cross is a word at war with all the playthings of the devil's clutter and clatter. We need the gospel constantly in our ears to create and recreate a space where grace rules. During the most devastating battles—as in the midst of divorce or at the bedside of a dying loved one—God's grace quiets the constant drumming of advertisements promising to make everything right; promising what they cannot deliver.

Finding My Own Story

I have three brothers all of whom are fine athletes. Growing up, we were a close-knit group who enjoyed playing football in our back yard. My two older siblings, Mark and Paul, played on their knees while my little brother Andy and I played on our feet. We played until someone got hurt.

I delighted in football, whether playing with my brothers in our backyard or watching the high school team play under the lights on Friday nights. The whole town showed up to cheer our team to victory, and I became convinced that performing well at sports would make me somebody. I persisted in this dream even after ending my third year of football with a cumulative 1 and 14 record. Tuition in the school of life, my mother called it.

I spent a lot of time wanting to become a good athlete like my brothers. Everyone called me "Little Ruge." The coaches, hoping I would be a late bloomer like my brothers, kept putting me on their teams. But I never bloomed. During JV basketball, my coach finally turned to me in practice one day and told me that I had the worst jump shot he had seen in thirty years of coaching. After the sting of his words wore off, I began to realize that athletic achievement wasn't a good way to define myself.

A year later, my father received a call to another congregation and we moved in the middle of my junior year of high school. I found myself in a new place where no one called me "Little Ruge" because they didn't know my big brothers. Minus the pressure to measure up to my brothers' athletic accomplishments I was free to explore the particular gifts God gave me. It was at this time that I discovered my love for performing magic and for performance in general. As emcee of the school talent show, I had my peers howling with laughter and I found it exhilarating to live out my own God-given identity instead of trying to shoehorn myself into another's. My mom always told my brothers and me, "You're each special in your own way." I finally believed it.

The expectation that I would succeed at sports had messed me up a bit. I was measuring myself against others' criteria that I could never satisfy. I simply did not have the resources within myself to meet that challenge. I learned through this experience that God's word of grace that comes to us through the cross meets each of us at a very personal level. While my struggles seem of little consequence amidst all the pain and brokenness in the lives of others and in the world, God's word affirming my worth and freeing me from the need to somehow measure up made a difference in my life. I have learned to focus on God and not on my own achievements.

Does the word of the cross have something to say to those whom the devil attacks with full frontal force? My personal experience with the world's evils does not equip me to answer this question. But I have witnessed the word of the cross do amazing things and have heard others witness to the grace they hear in it.

Stories of the Word in Times of Crisis

I am a biblical storyteller. I learn portions of the Bible by heart and then perform them in much the same way that the early church did. In chapter one the story based on the Gospel of Mark is based on my experiences as a storyteller. I now share the contemporary experiences that shaped that earlier story.

I once proclaimed Mark's version of the story of Jesus' death in a school classroom. I related how the crowds taunted, the sky darkened, and then Jesus called out from the cross, "My God, my God, why have you forsaken me?" As I cried out in the persona of Jesus, I noticed a woman crying. After class she came to me to explain what had happened to her in the hearing of the word of the cross. She told me that as a youth she had been held at knifepoint and raped repeatedly by someone she knew and trusted. "I always thought that God could not possibly understand what had happened to me. I felt that he had abandoned me when I needed him most. But just now when I heard Jesus crying out from the cross, 'My God, my God, why have you forsaken me?' I recognized that cry as my own and I knew that, in Jesus, God understood my horror."

Another time at a family retreat at Camp Chrysalis I noticed someone profoundly moved by Jesus' cry delivered through my lips. Later the woman—her name was Nancy—came to me to talk about her experience. She told me that the way I told the story, it appeared that Jesus could not see God when he cried out on the cross. "That is precisely what I believe happened," I responded. At that Nancy launched into her own story. She told me that her father had been a life-long Lutheran; a man of profound commitment who had raised her in the faith. But when his wife died, everything fell apart. He was plagued with doubt, and although he desired to believe in God, faith eluded him. He had died recently and, as far as Nancy knew, the dark clouds had never parted. "It's strange," she said, "but I find it comforting to know that Jesus died like my dad." In the middle of her own struggles with her father's doubt, some comfort came in knowing that Jesus had been there first.

Power in Weakness

The stories I've just told are amazing to me because it's at the point of God's ultimate vulnerability in the flesh and blood of Jesus that the power of God is revealed most clearly to these hurting women. I shouldn't be surprised. The Apostle Paul tells us that God's weakness is stronger than human strength (1 Cor. 1:25) and that the word of the cross is the power of God for those who are being saved (1 Cor. 1:18). And he goes on to claim that in Christ, God saves us weak, ungodly sinners who are enemies of God. In fact, God's love and grace are greatest precisely when we are least able to claim them (Rom. 5:6-10). God delivers love and grace to us by becoming one with us in our weakness, as we suffer the consequences of our sin. God comes to us in Jesus, revealing the power of love in a world that is drunk with the love of power.

Cross and resurrection are bound together. Death leads to life. The women we met in the previous stories discovered this to be true. They found their hopes raised by the one who died for them, then, secure in knowledge of God's love and forgiveness, they were free to comfort others who had suffered similar experiences. It is always the case that God meets us in our brokenness to bring us new life.

The world understands the means to power and glory to be through control, force, and domination. But in Jesus, the power of God is made perfect in weakness. While the world uses strength to demand our respect, Jesus empties himself and serves us, thereby inspiring our respect. Glory isn't in getting but giving. Power doesn't dominate others; it empowers them.

Where do we glimpse this kind of power in our own lives? I learned from my parent's relationship that the power of love is invitational not coercive. My mother didn't force my dad to be what she wanted him to be; she accepted him as he was. She won over my father's heart and in response to her love for him he grew to become the man he is today. As a pastor, my father didn't demand the respect of parishioners. He inspired their respect through his service to God and to God's people. The powerful influence the good people of Emmanuel had on my life was accomplished as much by their willingness to listen to me as by the words they shared—by their example of service more than their admonitions about the need to serve. They loved me from their vulnerabilities rather than their strengths, and they gave to me without expecting to receive from me in return. They modeled the Christ who comes as broken bread into the broken places of our lives where we hide abuse, failure, guilt, doubt, and shame. They impressed upon me the need to attend to such places in my own life, reminding me that if we run from our own failures, we may miss the healing presence of God. And if we are strangers to our own wounds and the wounds we have inflicted, how can we be compassionate in the presence of the wounds of others?

Attending to the Wounds of Others

Emmanuel Lutheran Church welcomed struggling people into the life of the congregation and offered them the opportunity to experience healing and wholeness in their hurting and fractured lives. On most nights of the week, Emmanuel hosted small groups of people who met regularly to provide counsel and care for one another. Some battled alcoholism, others obesity. Adult children who had grown up in dysfunctional families met to try and figure out healthier patterns of living for themselves and their families. Individuals whose spouses had died gathered to talk about the loved ones they had lost as well as their hopes and dreams for the future.

Every Thanksgiving Emmanuel provided a banquet for people who would otherwise spend the holiday alone. Hundreds came; some were hungry for food, others for fellowship. It made no difference to us. Jerry Thiex cooked up dozens of turkeys with all the trimmings. Others from the congregation set tables, served food, and washed mounds of dishes. Thinking of those gray November days spent wearing the servant's apron brings back some of my fondest Thanksgiving memories.

Our congregation embraced the Old Testament admonition to extend hospitality to the stranger, whether hungry and lonely neighbors or people from afar. Emmanuel joined three neighboring churches to welcome Pham Van Hau and his family into our community. We found them a place to live, supplied them with clothes, got their children into school, listened to their stories, and helped them adapt to a new country. Thankful for the love of God we enjoyed, we were moved to share that blessing with others. Remarkably, in the act of service, our lives were more profoundly blessed.

Welcoming strangers from across the sea into my part of the world was a new and exhilarating experience that broadened my understanding of the breadth of God's embrace. Little did I imagine that in a few short years I would be sent to serve an internship with the Lutheran Church in Chile. The realities I encountered there revealed to me how much bigger the world is than I ever imagined. As my world expanded, so did my understanding of the heights and depths and vastness of God's love. The word of the cross sounded in a new key for me.

For Further Thought

1. Who laid the foundations for your life of faith?

2. When have you encountered Christians who find their identity in God's demands rather than in God's divine gifts?

3. What new insights did you gain from this chapter that broaden your understanding of God's word of grace that comes to us through the cross? What experiences have you had that exemplify what you've learned?

4. Do Jesus' words, "My God, my God, why have you forsaken me," resonate with you? When have you felt abandoned? Who do you turn to in such times?

God is our refuge and strength, a very present help in trouble.
Therefore we will not fear—

Psalm 46:1-2a

4

The Word of the Cross in Latin America

Chile is a beautiful country on the western side of South America with miles and miles of ocean coast. Long and slim, it is made up of stark desert wilderness in the north, mountain ranges on its eastern border with Argentina, and snowy cold regions in the very south of the continent. Yet this beautiful country carries the scars of a violent history.

On September 11, 1973 (a day as much a part of Chilean national consciousness as our own 9/11) General Agusto Pinochet, backed by the CIA, overthrew the democratically elected president of Chile, Salvador Allende. Military planes flew at the Chilean presidential mansion spraying it with bullets. Thousands of Chileans who were seen as problematic to the new dictator were rounded up in the national stadium in Nunoa, Greater Santiago. Many did not live to tell about the atrocities that occurred there.

Prior to the coup of 1973, fishing was the way of life in Lo Rojas. From small family-owned boats just off shore, fishers caught enough fish to feed their families and to make a decent living. But Pinochet, eager to please those who helped put him in power—including the United States—embraced the wisdom of the Chicago School of Economics and opened Chilean waters to the international fishing industry. By the time I arrived fourteen years after the coup, foreign fishing companies were well established up and down the Chilean coast. Fleets of huge fishing boats over-fished the waters near shore, and factory waste that was discharged directly into the sea turned the water red with pollution. Local fishers, unable to reach the distant fishing fields or to pay for the fuel such trips required, couldn't compete.

While the industry made it possible for people in distant countries like the United States to purchase inexpensive Chilean salmon, it destroyed the local economy. Unemployment reached as high as eighty percent in the area where I lived in Lo Rojas. The factories Pinochet lured to Chilean shores to raise the national economy brought wealth for a few, but as one of the church council members in my congregation there wryly noted, "What is good for the Chilean economy does not seem to be so good for the Chileans!"

The cost of the glory was high. Lives were devoured. The persistent grind of poverty together with government-sponsored repression took a heavy toll. Relationships disintegrated. Health failed. Dreams turned to dust. Fear wedged itself between even the tightest embrace. Yet even as Pinochet boasted, with delusions of divinity, "Not a leaf in this country moves without my order!," the people celebrated the God of life who is with them in the shadow of death. They gave firm and faithful testimony to one who did not rule over them with an iron hand, but who went forth with them against all that would destroy them.

In August 1987 I began a pastoral internship with the good people of the Lutheran Church, San Pedro, in Coronel. For nearly two years I lived in a fishing sector of Chile called Lo Rojas and was part of a community of believers that included those baptized in Christ such as Anita, Ricardo, Estela, Pato, Elias, and Ximena. All had been touched by the war of terror that my country had backed in their land. Ximena lost many friends, Pato's father was murdered, and the others only hinted in hushed tones at the losses they had endured. Add these acts of personal violence to the economic destruction that the dictatorship inflicted on these faithful people.

Without romanticizing the people in any way, I confess that they held up for me the power and grace of the crucified Christ in the midst of a crucified people. Unlike the Psalmist, who laments "How could we sing the Lord's song in a foreign land?" I found that it seemed *more* fitting to sing the Lord's song in this strange land (Ps.137:4). In the people of Coronel, the word of the cross did as it had done in Corinth and among the baptized faithful under Roman occupation. The crucified Christ came and cried out with a crucified people in order that their agony might turn to alleluias. The violence hidden within the glories of the empire were laid bare, yet people hoped.

This is not to say that they offered an easy word for me to hear. I did not want to hear that the food stocked on grocery shelves at home left people in Chile hungry. I did not want to know that my government had brutally overthrown a democratically elected president. I had been taught that we fought for freedom and democracy, but our actions in Chile, in support of a brutal tyrant, seemed to have no purpose other than to protect crass economic advantages for our powerful nation. I saw that the products I enjoyed, like inexpensive fish, were paid for by the blood of my brothers and sisters in this place. Lo Rojas was the blood red wound on my own country's agenda, carefully hidden from our sight, so as not to call into question our own global vocation. Do we really seek to bring positive change to troubled areas of the world? Perhaps sometimes, but in the case of Chile the answer was that we did not.

I may have lost some readers with that accusation. We like to think of our nation's efforts and legacy as noble and just. I was able to endure the accusation—the condemning voice of the law—because those who reluctantly laid the truth before me did so while welcoming me enthusiastically and loving me fiercely. From the day that I arrived, they opened their hearts to me and endured my faltering Spanish. "He's just speaking the way he does. What he means is…" Ximena would say, translating my broken Spanish into something intelligible. They fed me and invited me into their homes. They threw a party to celebrate my mother's milestone birthday when my parents came to visit. They danced her around the room, living out the wisdom of another Latin American, Otto Maduro, who once told me, "Life is so fragile we must celebrate it!" They asked me to baptize their children and allowed me the privilege of burying their dead.

The wide embrace of the Chilean people allowed me to stare down the demons of my country's relationship with theirs. I relearned the lesson I had learned in Menominee—God's love is as wide as the world in which I live—a world much wider than I had imagined possible. As my world got larger, so did my sense of God's grace. The God who held me in my baptism now held me together with brothers and sisters from across the world. This same God who held me accountable to my past also embraced me with the loving arms of Christ's body on earth.

The Sustaining Word of the Cross

I discovered very quickly that the Chilean Christians leaned heavily on God's word of grace in the cross of Jesus to sustain them in their daily lives—lives that were intimately familiar with poverty and fear. In this word they heard that the God revealed in Jesus Christ is a God who comes out in their favor. They understood themselves to be God's "beloved children," an identity that emboldened them amidst the threats around them. The word of the cross assured them that God hears their cries and sees their suffering; that in Jesus Christ God comes down and meets them in the places they live and in the places where death threatens. God comes caring for their needs, feeding their hungers, binding up their wounds, forgiving their sins, and making them into a new community. Jesus, who has known death, promises to bring them new life today and forever. To an oppressed people accustomed to having very little, this quiet but dramatic word of hope spoken through the lips of the community of faith provided sustenance as life-giving as daily bread. In the pages to come you will meet several speakers of this good word.

The Word Spoken by Estela

Estela was the president of the congregation when I first arrived in Chile. About forty years of age, she was the mother of several children and grandmother of one, all of whom lived with her in a very small house. Estela rarely had a quiet moment to herself, yet she found time to visit people in need and care for them. She was part of the women's Bible study group at San Pedro and one day she shared a dream she had had about Marta, a woman who had attended the group for a time but then stopped coming.

In Estela's dream Marta was trapped in mud up to her waist; a situation that Estela thought was funny because Marta looked like a child playing in the mud. "No, I am stuck. I can't get out!" Marta cried out. Realizing that she truly needed help, Estela tried desperately to free Marta and ended up getting stuck herself.

"It was terrible," Estela announced to the study group, "we thought we were lost. Then, suddenly, all of you appeared. You made a chain with your hands and you leaned back and pulled as hard as you could until you pulled us both to solid ground."

After hearing the account of Estela's dream, the women in the study group decided that they had been called to find Marta and to bring her back to solid ground—the solid ground of Bible study and the community of support in place around it. They moved outside the comfort of being together to study God's word in order to bear a word of reconciliation and hope to a sister in need, just as Jesus had done for each of them on the cross.

Given all the challenges she faced each day and the demands on her time and energy, I once asked Estela what brought her to church? She replied that she appreciated the silence. In the quiet moments before the worship service begins, she told me that she sits beneath the cross and prays to God, pouring out her sorrows and gaining strength for the week ahead. She knows that when no one else pays attention to her, God hears her cries and will not fail her. In the silence she hears God speak. In the community of Christ she is comforted and empowered.

The Word Spoken by the Arpillera Women

Another group of Chilean women from a community several miles away also invited me into their life. These women gathered in the Lutheran day care to make *arpilleras*, which are small tapestries made out of scraps of cloth, depicting daily life in Chile or stories from the Bible. While they sewed, the women talked about issues with their husbands or the latest "reforms" of Pinochet and the effects on their communities. They shared their dreams for their children, many of whom played nearby as their mothers stitched and talked.

The women gathered together and made works of art to send throughout the world to tell their own stories and the grand story of God's redemption of creation. They counted on one another to help mend broken hearts and spirits; to help stitch their lives back together. They took the scraps sent to them by the "First World" and turned them into testimonies of beauty that they sold to raise money for the day care and to provide resources to attend to need of their own families.

The faith of the arpillera women is deep and rich. The tapestries they create tell the stories about Jesus who prior to his death on the cross traveled throughout Galilee healing the sick, feeding the hungry, and bringing a word of hope and empowerment to poor people like themselves. Yes, the arpillera women know the stories about Jesus, but more importantly they know Jesus; they know his love for them. They live in the promise that God's glory is revealed when the humble are uplifted.

After the coup in 1973, the Lutheran church in Chile experienced a major rupture. Some Lutheran congregations were comprised almost exclusively of Chileans who had come from Germany and who still spoke German as their primary language. Other German Chilean churches made an effort to start communities like San Pedro in Lo Rojas where I served. The German-speaking congregations tended to see Pinochet in a very positive light. But San Pedro's sponsoring congregation, a community of faith that had been served by Helmut Frenz, the president of the Evangelical Lutheran Church in Chile at the time of the political coup, and later by my supervisory pastor, Konrad Schulz, had a distinctive experience.

At first Pastor Frenz had supported Pinochet, hoping that he might quickly restore order in the country following the takeover. When it became clear, however, that Pinochet and his violent methods to exercise power were the new order of the day, Frenz took a firm stand. His evangelical voice called on Pinochet to stop crucifying the people of Chile. In response Frenz received death threats and ended up having to flee the country for his own safety. Eventually, the Lutherans who supported Pinochet split off and formed their own Lutheran denomination. Their political conservatism led to theological conservatism that, in my opinion, moved them away from the gospel heritage back toward the law. That is the context; now here is the story.

The Word Spoken by Konrad Schulz

During my internship, I had occasion to go with my supervisor, Pastor Konrad Schulz, and several youth from the congregation to a youth event sponsored by the new Lutheran denomination formed after the coup. While there was mention of the gospel, I realized quickly that law, not gospel, was the theme proclaimed most often from the pulpit at the camp where the event was held. Listening to the litany of what Christians do not do, I easily imagined myself in the church of my father's youth where the message of *NO!* was proclaimed frequently and loudly. By midweek my supervisor and I had grown tired of the leaders spiritually beating up the kids.

One day as worship was about to begin, the worship leader announced, "We worship the one Holy God, source of all that is. If you cannot do this with your whole heart, if you cannot give yourself fully to God, then we offer you this opportunity to get up and leave right now."

Taken aback by what seemed to me to be a kind of altar call in reverse, I turned to look at my supervisor. But Pastor Schulz had finally had all he could stand. Raising himself up in front of the group gathered for worship—all six feet two of him—he announced in a very loud voice, "I'm leaving with the sinners!" With that he stormed out.

After Pastor Schulz' unceremonious exit, the room came alive with energy. The youth wanted to understand what has just happened. "What did he say?" some asked. "Why did he say that?" others wondered. "Do you think we can leave too?" It felt to me like the Spirit has descended upon us and was filling the place with excitement and true seeking after God. For the first time all week, young people were engaged in lively conversation about matters of faith.

But the leadership would have none of it. They made everyone settle down and forced us to sing a Spanish equivalent of "Kumbayah." I remember thinking how ironic it was that the song they chose was a prayer inviting God to come to us but that we were required to sing in order to *drive out* the enlivening spirit who had entered the room.

Pastor Schulz spoke that night and in doing so embodied the word of the cross. He put flesh on a God who chooses to go with sinners rather than listen to the prayers of those who think themselves righteous. He reminded us that the glory of God is not found in judgmental attitudes and spiritual domination. The glory of God leaves with sinners.

Transition Home

My return home was difficult. I had experienced the word of the cross profoundly, both spoken and embodied by my Chilean brothers and sisters. I had met Christ crucified walking among an oppressed people. I had come to understand more deeply that glory as defined by my homeland has nothing to do with the glory that is God's.

During my time in Chile, I witnessed how Christ comes to people in pain to rescue them and carry them as a community to freedom; how God stitches us all back together and travels with us from our places of safety into a world in need. I'd heard God in the voice of Helmut Frenz publicly crying out against repression; and more intimately in the voices of the *arpillera* women speaking life to each other. In Chile, my world expanded, my awareness of the body of Christ grew, and my trust in the vastness of Christ's loving solidarity blossomed.

When I landed in Miami, I turned on the television and saw a program about body builders for Jesus. I watched as they flexed their exaggerated muscles, witnessing to a crowd of screaming fans about the pecs and abs God had given them as reward for their faithfulness. With their powerful bodies they were able to break beams as thick as telephone poles with their bare hands. This exhibition of raw power was something to behold, but it had nothing to do with the power of Christ—power that strengthens hearts and opens clenched hands to better serve others. After all that I had witnessed and experienced among the weak and vulnerable in Chile, I was incensed at the claim that God's blessing was in any way connected with the power that strutted across the television screen. What blatant misuse of God's name!

The power of God is not human power on steroids; God's power challenges our body-building values and our very conception of power. God's glory is not in human magnificence and strength. The glory of God is fragile and broken. God's power truly is made perfect in weakness. Jesus promises, embodies, and draws us into this fragile glory as he comes down again to be among a people desperately needing a gospel word.

The Word of the Cross among Refugees

In 1990 I was called to serve a congregation of Spanish-speaking people on Long Island in New York. A majority of our members were from El Salvador, a country torn apart by a long and bloody civil war. Many were immigrants who found themselves in the awkward position of fleeing from violence in their homeland to the very country that provided financial support for the war that forced them to leave. Ironically, the peaceful presence of these people in the United States provided a counter-balance to the violence that our country exported to their country. Working at hard labor for long hours, this industrious people saved money to send to loved ones back home who lived in poverty and the fear of death. The money exported by these refugees made up a goodly portion of El Salvador's national income. These good Christian people, including a man named Daniel, taught me about the word of the cross in their lives.

The Word Spoken by Daniel

In his early twenties Daniel learned that the gospel of Jesus Christ calls for all Christians to take up their cross and follow him. For Daniel this meant working with those who are internal refugees in his home country; living with and helping sustain the men, women, and children displaced by the civil war. The powers and principalities pursued these innocent people, fearing that if they were permitted to gather together in one place they would share the stories of the violence done to them with each other and with the world. Still, Daniel persisted in his efforts to follow Jesus wherever he leads.

One day Jesus lead Daniel and a rag-tag group of refugees to Chalatenango. Mothers and children, the elderly, and pregnant women found a place to sleep in the church of Refuge of *Doña María*. Daniel chose to sleep on the floor under the altar and leave the pews to the others. During the night all were awakened by the blast of a bomb that had been placed in the church entryway by the military. Daniel responded instinctively and wisely, instructing mothers to cover the mouths of their children to keep them quiet as he lead the terrified group of people on a midnight journey to where the humanitarian organization, the Green Cross, was encamped. It grieved Daniel deeply to see those who could barely walk shuffling away in fear and shock, displaced one more time. But he knew he had to get them to safety. Luckily they escaped the church before two more bombs went off.

In caring for others Daniel put his own life at risk. No one forced him to do what he did. Daniel chose this path because he heard Jesus' call to take up his cross and follow; to seek life in the face of death and to stand with those who suffer in order to bring them life.

Daniel loves the Lutheran church. There he learned of the God who, in Jesus, comes to people, hears their cries, touches their reality, lives their fear, and brings them liberation. The exodus that the people of Israel experienced isn't past history, Daniel insists. The liberty to the captives that Jesus announced was not just for Galilee or heaven. "We are living it now," he once told me.

The strength of this conviction was tested when Daniel was arrested and tortured without trial. His captors drenched him with water and applied electric shock to his most sensitive body parts. They tried to convince him that they were the gods he should obey. But Daniel refused to renounce his faith in Christ Jesus. In the midst of excruciating pain, he found consolation and strength in knowing that Jesus, too, had endured torture and death. Just as his Lord suffered before him, Daniel suffered for his commitment to a just cause. His horrific story is woven into the broader narrative of God's commitment to the world that is revealed in the incarnate word of the cross. In the end, resurrection and life will have the final word—even in war-torn countries.

A Mighty Fortress

Because of my experiences in Chile and with my Salvadoran congregation I wonder what the gospel I was introduced to as a child has to do with the gospel they know. Because I am Lutheran I wonder what Luther's testimony has to say in the context of their lives of faith.

A Salvadoran refugee named William provided music for our worship services at our church in New York. Once when we were practicing Luther's hymn, "A Mighty Fortress Is Our God," for a Reformation service, William announced that the hymn brought back memories for him. "Pastor, this song was sung at funeral services I attended for those murdered by the death squads," he told me. "When we sang it, we knew who 'the hordes of devils threatening to devour us' were."[1]

In Luther's theology and music, those gathered in the shadow of death hear a voice that names evil by its proper name. But it also speaks of One who enters the shadow of death with them in order to conquer the power of death. The God who comes in Jesus comes to save them from the evil that threatens and attacks. God sees them as they are and chooses them to become servants of the gospel of life. The crucified One brings life into the shadow of death, empowering those who suffer to rise again.

This is the glory of God.

Every Good Friday, this congregation of refugees on New York's Long Island participates with other Christians from throughout the community in the Way of the Cross—a reenactment of the trial and death of Jesus. The majority of the participants don't play specific roles; they simply walk together with Jesus toward his death. Like Jesus these people know the cost of being tried unfairly and judged too quickly. They know what it is like to be taunted and to be condemned to die. On this day, their walk with Jesus is a confession of their faith that he walks with them in their struggles, both personal and communal. Together they walk in the glory of God.

For Further Thought

1. How has this testimony arising from Latin America challenged you or helped you see new dimensions of the gospel?

2. What does the word of the cross say to those faced with the terror of "hordes of devils"?

3. The quest for wealth or influence by one people or nation can lead to violence against another. What examples do you see of this in the world today?

4. What does the crucified Christ bid us to do in a world where the privileges of some are paid for by the sweat and blood of many?

If any want to become my followers, let them deny themselves and take up their cross and follow me. For those who want to save their life will lose it, and those who lose their life for my sake, and for the sake of the gospel, will save it.

Mark 8:34-35

5

The Word of the Cross in a World of Glory

Jesus' incarnation continues to challenge us today as the church proclaims the word of the cross. We understand that not only Jesus' death but the whole of his life was filled with a passion to bring new life to others. The new life Jesus offers us through this strange word of the cross draws our lives into its offbeat rhythms. Once Jesus' way of seeing grasps us, our lives conform to the cross-shaped pattern of his life.

Through the pages of this book, we overheard the word of the cross spoken through the centuries in particular places around the world. First, in scripture Paul's letter proclaiming the word of the cross confronted a divided community of believers in Corinth, challenging them to see beyond the powers that divided them to the greater power that enabled their life together. Later, Mark's Gospel connected the word of the cross with those who lost temple, homeland, and loved ones by announcing the suffering solidarity of God in Jesus Christ. In his ministry Jesus brought healing to the broken. In death he was hanged in a place all too familiar to those who lived under Roman occupation. In his resurrection life triumphed over death.

Many centuries later, a conversation in Reformation Germany offered assurance to the poor and lowly that the word of the cross in Jesus guarantees that God acts graciously for God's people. Word of God's respect for those of little regard and God's love for those who are otherwise unloved turned the world upside down. This theme carried over into the chapter on middle America, where we heard how the word of the cross brings forgiveness and new life to those transformed by Jesus' self-giving love. This act of self-giving reveals true power in weakness.

And finally we heard how those in situations of intense political persecution experienced the living God calling them to lives of community and service. Each of these experiences of God's gracious transformation through the word of the cross is grounded in Jesus' ministry, death, and resurrection. But how are these various hearings of the word of the cross connected? What impact do they have on each of us in our very divided world? To answer these questions, we turn to another story from the Gospel of Mark.

Jesus Heals Two Women

A religious leader, a man of power and status in his community, a man with a name—Jairus—seeks out Jesus. Jairus is desperate because his daughter is very sick. He comes to Jesus and falls at his feet, pleading for his daughter's life. (This humble act makes him the first religious leader in Mark's Gospel to model faith.)

Jesus goes with Jairus and a huge crowd follows. Among the throng of people is a woman who has spent all of her money on doctors trying to stop the flow of blood that she has suffered for twelve years. As she makes her way toward Jesus, people move quickly to get out of her way. Her infirmity is known to many and, according to religious law, renders her unclean. Her ritual impurity excludes her from the human interactions of daily life. She must remain on the edges of her society, separated from strangers and family alike.

The woman knows that she shouldn't be here, that she shouldn't do what she is about to do. But she is desperate. She has heard of Jesus' power to heal and she believes with all her heart that if she can touch even the hem of his robe, she will be healed and will be able to return to the community and the life she was forced to leave behind a dozen years earlier.

And so when the opportunity arises, she reaches out her hand and touches Jesus' cloak, drawing on his power, and at the same time, rendering him unclean through her touch. It is an act of great courage and grave transgression. And she is healed immediately.

Jesus turns to see who has touched him, to see whom his power has entered. She hides, but Jesus takes the time to hunt for her even though his disciples advise otherwise. Jairus must have wanted to scream, "You're on an urgent mission, Jesus! My daughter is dying! This unclean woman has suffered for twelve years. Have her make an appointment and deal with her tomorrow." But Jesus seeks her out then and there, and when he finds her she falls at his feet—just as Jairus did a little while earlier. Jesus raises her up and declares that her faith has healed her.

While Jesus gazes into her eyes and pats her hands, people come from Jairus' house and find this important religious leader waiting helplessly while Jesus wastes precious time on a woman they know is unclean. They break the tragic news to Jairus that his daughter has died and tell him to leave the unclean teacher behind. But Jesus raises up the healed woman as example and tells Jairus to be like her, "Don't be afraid; trust courageously!"

Then Jesus and a handful of his followers accompany Jairus to his home. They are welcomed with the sound of loud lamenting. When Jesus assures them that the girl will live, the mourners mock him. Word of his soiled reputation has preceded him. He responds by throwing them out of the house. Then Jesus goes to this second daughter of Israel and raises her to life. Amazingly, as the twelve-year-old girl walks about, Jesus tells her parents—weeping with joy and wonder—not to mention the incident to anyone.

Right! I'm sure none of the funeral guests will need an explanation!

Two Healings, One Story

At first glance these verses tell two healing stories: Jesus restores a faith-filled woman to health and life in community and raises a dead girl to life again. But woven together as they are, the two stories say much more. The fate of the daughter of Jairus is linked to the fate of the woman who trusts courageously. The two already are bound together in strange ways. The number of years the woman has suffered matches the age of the girl. The woman's bodily function that has gone awry is the same bodily function the twelve year old is about to begin experiencing. Jairus seeks help for his daughter; Jesus welcomes the woman as "daughter." Both Jairus and the woman fall at Jesus' feet and both ultimately exhibit great trust in Jesus. Remarkably, the fate of those at the center of the social and religious community connects to the fate of the one who is relegated to the edge of community.

Jesus holds these two lives together. He is the agent of life for both women.

Jairus is aware of his own pain, but he finds healing only when he is willing to follow Jesus along the edges of his community to places he would not have gone on his own. If Jairus had abandoned Jesus when the "wrong" person appeared, the lament would not have departed his home. But Jairus stays with Jesus and learns from the unclean woman. Jesus commends the woman for her faith and calls on Jairus to have such faith. Jairus, the man at the center of society, must trust courageously like the woman who lives at the edges.

When Jairus models his response after the woman's, healing comes to his house. But more importantly, Jesus heals the broken community so that once again Israel can embrace both daughters. The family of God in its fullness comes together in the wedded healing of these two daughters of Israel. Touched by the unclean woman, Jesus becomes like the least and invites Jairus to walk into resurrection with him. The cross is that ultimate place of rejection where Jesus enters whole-heartedly, broken-heartedly, in order to bring life to those far off and those near. In the cross, Paul insists, Jesus completes what he embodies in the whole life story of God's people. Jesus breaks down the walls of hostility between us and them, creating a new, united people. Let us go back to some of the places visited earlier in this book and consider them in light of this story.

A Journey for Today's Jairus

This story models for us what being crucified and raised with Jesus means. Like Jairus, we need to become aware of the brokenness that haunts us. We need to be aware of the ways death slithers into our homes: as distorted ideas about people unlike ourselves, as consumerism that does not bring life, as feigned certainty amidst questions and doubt. When we bring this brokenness to Jesus, he does not rush to our homes to set things in order. Rather, he takes us on a timely detour to where others are suffering; to places we normally wouldn't go. In the presence of a raped student, an abused child, a grieving friend, a shattered community, a tortured human being, we begin to learn what healing and courageous faith—resurrection—might look like for us. We begin to trust that for us healing will happen when we mirror Jesus' concern for those more vulnerable than we.

Jesus' passion for the broken ones is made concrete in his lived word of the cross. Death on a wooden cross is the price the world charged him for his life among outcast people. Jesus' cross-shaped life redefines glory as divine suffering presence on a quest for radical transformation. Since we, as God's people, are invited into this process of radical transformation, let's examine four steps in the process powerfully captured in the story of these two healings.

Step One: Acknowledge Our Own Pain

If we do not attend to our own woundedness, we will not recognize how important it is that we begin our journey toward resurrection and transformation. Jairus' concern for his daughter interrupts his life, bringing him close to Jesus and the courageously trusting woman. Once he attends to his own pain, he can connect with the pain of another. In the process he embarks on his life-giving journey of transformation.

A few years ago I found myself beginning such a journey. People whom I had trusted acted with utter disregard for someone I loved. Every time I saw them, anger festered within me. I shouted my anger, but I did not know the name of my pain. I was invited into a week of healing called Concentric Journeys. Our facilitator, David Doerfler, used paths of healing that had been developed out of intense, reconciliation work. David brought together those who had lost loved ones to violent crimes and the imprisoned perpetrators of the crimes so that brutally honest but life-giving conversations could occur. Wounded people healed; wounding people healed; rips in the fabric of our community healed in wondrous ways. Resurrection happened. Getting to a place of such miraculous encounter required the intense attentiveness of the participants and the facilitator. But the healing of brokenness, shame, and bitterness emerged from the careful conversations between the persons lamenting their losses and the persons who had attacked them. New life was born.

During my week with Concentric Journeys, the methods that led to the healings of perpetrators and survivors alike began in me a journey toward healing for my own personal pain and shame. I found that being listened to compassionately as I told my tale of woe opened my heart. And I, in turn, listened to other wounded, yet healing, people. We held the pain together in our group so that transformation could begin. In touch with my own pain, shame, and even guilt, I was less obsessed with myself and more concerned about new life for others, who had, in fact, suffered much more than I had. I cannot say enough about how powerful it was to have the participants take my suffering seriously and "listen" me into new life.

Life is filled with pain. Pain caused by the guilt of sins we've committed; shame foisted upon us by another's act against us; the failure of failed promises of consumption and prosperity, or from the self-knowledge that our successes are really a sham. If we run from the pain in our lives, we will never make it to a place where new life is possible.

Step Two: Visit the Edges

Once we acknowledge our own pain, we are ready to take our pain to Jesus. Trusting in his promise of healing, we set out with him on the course he determines we must travel. For those of us at the center of power and privilege, healing usually comes when we join Jesus on a detour to the edges. There we learn how brutal brokenness can be and how beautiful faith is. When we travel with Jesus, he takes us to places we cannot even imagine. Walking with him on unfamiliar ground nurtures humility in us. As we enter into the life of the other, we confront how little we actually know; we recognize that our carefully organized world does not account for all that is.

Jairus knew he could do nothing to help his daughter by himself so he leaned on Jesus. In the process he learned a great deal about his own place of privilege as a leader in his religious community. Being a privileged person protects one from ever having to think about one's privilege. Although the world of privilege is arranged to keep people like Jairus in blissful ignorance of the plight of others less fortunate than themselves, Jesus shoves reality into our faces. Encountering the woman on the margins, Jairus meets the suffering he and his community inflict on others, but he also glimpses a courageous trust to model in his own life. Here again the same Jesus who was pushed to the edge of the cosmos and up onto a cross walks in edgy ways. Hanging out where demons tread, where widows are exploited, where pain cries out for healing, Jesus brings life. Remember Jesus' promise to his disciples: "The poor you will always have with you." He is not asserting a fatalistic, "Poverty is permanent, get used to it." Rather he speaks of the character of the community called by his name: "Since you are my disciples, of course you will always be with the people whom I have spent a lifetime loving, the poor."[1]

Jesus invites us to travel with him through broken places and attend to the wounded people who dwell there. While we may lose certain privileges as we take several steps away from the glory offered us by the world, traveling this path allows us access to the true community and identity we long for. In this journey, we cease to invest in that which does not satisfy. We discover the bread of life that truly meets our most intimate needs. This was my experience among the people of Chile and El Salvador. They showed me elements of my reality that had been hidden from my sight, and they did so without condemnation. They shared their stories and they loved me. But we cannot demand or expect such generosity from those whose suffering we cause. We cannot demand and expect reconciliation before the encounter even begins. But I must say that again and again I have experienced this love and welcome among those who are on the margins. While they have every right to be angry and seek revenge, those whom I have encountered have chosen to go a still more excellent way.

The hospitality of welcome and forgiveness is the fruit of our journey with Jesus to the edges. While speaking at my university about her community's commitment to the margins, Jenny Case, a legal defender of the indigent, made the accurate observation that those with privilege must initiate the contact between the divided groups. This is an important insight. Because of the flow of blood, the unclean woman could not go to synagogue to meet Jairus. A lack of resources made it impossible for the people of Chile to travel to the United States to be with the Christian community here. And people who are homeless may well find themselves pursued by the law if they attempt to enter into my neighborhood to meet me. Since those on the edges cannot come to us, we must travel to them to hear their stories, enter into solidarity with them, and learn from them about God's more excellent way.

Jesus calls us to the edges with him, insisting that we trust him to sustain us on this journey. When I was in seminary, I met a woman who had worked for many years with people who are homeless. Eventually she realized that while the support system of which she was part was well intended, it wasn't changing people's lives. So she decided to relocate herself on the edges. She sold everything she had and asked friends to sustain her at the poverty level with their monthly financial support. During the day, she opened her small apartment to her former clients who soon became her friends. She gave them a space to let their guard down and be with others in conversation and healthy community. She provided a safe place for them to see visions and dream dreams. Did the change she made make a difference? She claimed that in her new life, poor as she was, she felt richer that ever before. And those who received her hospitality testified to the resurrection worked in their lives.

The word of the cross is not just doctrine, though it is grounded in doctrine. It is not a theory about what happened between God and Jesus on the cross, although that event shapes it radically. Above all, the word of the cross is a way of seeing the world from the perspective of the brokenness caused by our quests for glory. The word of the cross offers us a new way of being in the world with others. We move to the edges to acknowledge that given the failures of the systems we've erected to provide care for disenfranchised people (and hide them from our view), we have been called to work together to build a better future for the whole community, not only people of means and privilege.

Step Three: Embrace the Link

Our own suffering and the suffering of those we encounter on the edges are linked. For instance, North Americans' obsession with driving fancy, new-model vehicles purchased at a reasonable price fuels the outsourcing of labor to foreign manufacturers who can deliver the goods for significantly less money than domestic manufacturers can. As a consequence, American manufacturers who pay their workers a decent wage and provide safe working conditions can't compete and are forced to lay-off workers and even close plants, which contributes to growing unemployment and poverty in this country. Sadly, our desire to drive vehicles that project an image of status and power satisfies neither our deep needs for a true sense of worth nor the basic needs of laborers at home and in distant places.

Our national security is bound up in the violence we effect in other parts of the world, whether Chile, El Salvador, or another country we label as evil. Closer to home, we feel safe only when we lock out those we perceive to threaten our way of life. (Shouldn't we feel safest when we *aren't* locking our gates?) In comparison to so many others, we are wealthy and secure beyond belief. It's appropriate for us to celebrate our blessings—to give thanks for what we have been given—but we must constantly ask if what we have is *God's* gift to us or blessings we have stolen from others on the margins. And in order to have the wisdom to know the difference between divine blessings and stolen goods, we need to listen to people on the margins. They see what we are not able to see; they know what we must come to know.

Sometimes we exclude from our worship people who remind us of our own economic insecurity, questionable morals, or personal failures. We squelch our children's questions about why things are the way they are because we wonder the same thing, and it scares us. Denying our doubts, our duplicity, and our indebtedness to systems that work in our favor so that we can continue on our merry way requires that we disregard all who will not embrace our perspective. Only when we are able to see ourselves as others see us can we move toward a new and better life for the whole of God's creation.

Regular contact with the people on the edges is necessary. The word of the cross is not something we can attend to briefly and then return to our happy lives. During a recent eye exam, my optometrist told me that I had a minor astigmatism in one eye. He said he could correct it with glasses, but that I would have to commit to wearing the glasses all of the time. "Otherwise when you wear the glasses you will see things as they are, but your mind will insist that your new vision is a distortion. It will stick to what it thinks it knows. Only by constantly looking through the corrective lens will your mind learn to see things as they really are." And so it is with the word of the cross. If we slip it on to see the world for an hour on Sunday, we will continue in our distorted vision so that when we glimpse the truth it will look like a lie. Jesus promises in the word of the cross nothing less than death and nothing more than a glorious new life. All things are made new as we see and live in the new reality Jesus reveals to us.

Step Four: Live the Good News

I'm sure that Jairus did not regret his journey. After all, his life was transformed because of it. He experienced not only the resurrection of his daughter but also his own resurrection. Our journey with Jesus will not always be a "good time," but the gift we receive in walking with Jesus to the edges is definitely good news. Jairus' world expanded as a result of the journey he made. He learned that the love and faithfulness of God he experienced at home and at worship also extends to people on the edges—further, I'm sure, than he imagined possible.

I believe that Jesus invites each of us on a journey, a detour to the edges. I had the privilege of journeying with Spanish-speaking people for many years and in those encounters Jesus gave me new life and a new way of looking at all of life. He has done the same for others I know, and, as you can see from their lives, the possibilities for where

Jesus takes us in service to others are endless: Tim proclaims the gospel in Spanish. Taryn finds herself working against violence in Africa. Brian's heart is captive to feeding hungry people. Weldon uses his trip to Iraq to discern the things that make for peace. Annette and Eric seek the healing of creation's wounds, mending the world that we have broken. Chris helps us understand the pain that our hatred brings to others. Jaime plants a garden for people who are homeless. Emily works with gay and lesbian Christians who have been excluded from our communities of faith much as the unclean woman was excluded from Jairus's community. Heather attends to youth who are wondering where in the world they can find hope. Norm repairs century-old wounds between Christians and Jews. Andrea cares for elderly adults whose savings aren't sufficient to sustain them in old age. Jason explores new rhythms of life in the disharmony of the world. Gayle leads college students to consider the roots of our society's problems. Peter shares coffee and conversation with people who are homeless. David comforts those weighed down by shame. Mariana photographs children whose faces we might otherwise not see. Sister Helen visits prisons to unleash the power of the gospel among people waiting to be executed. In the process we learn to love sinners—including ourselves.

My wife and I are committed to embracing an alternative way of ordering our life that is modeled on Jesus' way. Every day presents new challenges *and* new insights as Lori and I and our children, Lucas and Luisa, walk together with Jesus into the future, buoyed by a hope that does not disappoint.

If you let him, Jesus will take you on a journey to a place you don't expect and with an itinerary that is vastly different than you had planned. Be humble on your journey, open to hearing the word of the cross from unexpected people. Pay careful attention to those excluded from your own religious community, those identified as unclean, those invisible to the world's glory.

Jesus embodies God's glory—the simple yet divine self-giving bread. The meal that Jesus offers us costs us nothing, but it satisfies us fully. In this meal we receive far more than a bit of bread and a sip of wine; we are welcomed into community, empowered with courageous trust, and provided with life itself. In the breaking of the bread, the crucified and resurrected Jesus raises us up to walk in newness of life—a life lived in service to others and to their benefit, not only our own. This life poured out to the world is our grateful response to the God who grants us life today and forever.

For Further Thought

1. With whom do you identify in the story of two healings?

2. What connections do you see between your privilege and others' brokenness? Between your brokenness and others' privilege?

3. With what specific group on the margins is Jesus telling you to walk? How can you structure your life to have regular contact with them?

4. In what ways have/will the cross and resurrection of Jesus radically transform your way of seeing the world and living in it?

Notes

Chapter 1

1. Apollos is introduced in Acts 18:24-26 as a Jew, a native of Alexandria, who knew the scriptures inside and out and was passionate about proclaiming Jesus as the long-awaited Messiah. He was tutored by Priscilla and Aquila in Ephesus and later traveled to Corinth, where he became an effective church leader. 1 Corinthians 16:12 seems to indicate that Apollos was with Paul when Paul wrote his letter to the Corinthians, and Paul encouraged him to return to Corinth but Apollos declined to do so at the time.

2. Cephus is better known as Peter, Jesus' disciple.

3. This is the last verse in the oldest manuscripts of Mark's Gospel. Some later manuscripts add other details of Jesus' resurrection to tidy things up and harmonize Mark's account with that of the other Gospels.

Chapter 2

1. These dialogues are based on careful research into these texts in their historical context. See my book, *Cross in Tension* (Pickwick, 2008).

2. Luther's *Ninety-Five Theses* are included in Luther's Works volume 31.

3. The *Heidelberg Disputation* is in Luther's Works volume 31.

4. See *The Blessed Sacrament* Luther's Works volume 35 for Luther's sermon on the Lord's Supper.

5. Luther's commentary on the Magnificat is in Luther's Works volume 21.

6. This is a paraphrase of Luke 1:52-53.

7. This pamphlet is on the internet at http://www.pitts.emory.edu/dia/1521LuthWWBook/pc1.cfm.

Chapter 4

1. *Evangelical Lutheran Worship* (Minneapolis: Augsburg Fortress, Publishers, 2006), 503, 504. The third verse of the hymn begins, "Though hordes of devils fill the land all threat'ning to devour us."

Chapter 5

1. See Mark 14:3-9.

For Further Reading

On St. Paul's Theology of the Cross
Picket, Ray. *The Cross in Corinth: The Social Significance of the Death of Jesus* (Sheffield, Eng.: Sheffield Academic, 1997).

On Interpreting Mark's Gospel
Rhoads, David with Joanna Dewey and Donald Michie. *Mark as Story: An Introduction to the Narrative of the Gospel,* Second edition, (Minneapolis: Fortress Press, 1999).

On Luther's Message in His Social Context
Ruge-Jones, Philip. *Cross in Tensions: Theology of the Cross as Politico-social Critique* (Eugene, Ore.: Pickwick, 2008).

On Luther's Word of the Cross as Grace
Forde, Gerhard O. *Where God Meets Man: Luther's Down-to-Earth Approach to the Gospel* (Minneapolis: Augsburg Publishing House, 1972).

On the Word of the Cross in the Midst of a Crucified People
Tesfai, Yacob. *The Scandal of a Crucified World: Perspectives on the Cross and Suffering* (Maryknoll, N.Y.: Orbis, 1994).

On the Theology of the Cross as a Lens for Interpreting the World
Solberg, Mary M. *Compelling Knowledge: A Feminist Proposal for an Epistemology of the Cross* (Albany: SUNY Press, 1997).

On the Theology of the Cross as a Way of Living in the World

Westhelle, Vítor. *The Scandalous God: The Use and Abuse of the Cross* (Minneapolis: Fortress Press, 2006).

On Living Faithfully toward Transformation with Those on the Margins

Wallis, Jim. *Faith Works: How to Live Your Beliefs and Ignite Positive Social Change* (New York: Random House, 2005).